Praise

'Elaine is a home-staging expert who uses science and highly-credible research to inform her professional work. Her book is a masterpiece of expert advice, straight from her own experience as a highly-respected, professional home-stager. She has been incredibly generous with her expertise and has presented it in an easy to access and informative format. A must-have for every home-mover.'

—**Jayne Dowle**, freelance homes and property journalist

'Elaine is one of a kind. Extremely experienced, diligent and professional, she is a source of invaluable knowledge and committed to inspire others. In her own refined way, she shares her immeasurable knowledge and her views on property marketing, making this book a must-read for anyone looking to deepen their understanding of how to sell their home well.'

— **Paloma Harrington-Griffin**, Founding Director of the Home Staging Association UK & Ireland and Vice President of the IAHSP® Europe (International Association of Home Staging Professionals Europe)

'This is an absolute must-read for anyone selling property and looking to get the best possible price. Elaine has written something unique, which is conversational in its style so you feel like you're having a coffee with her and she is imparting her knowledge to you. It is easy to read and has fantastic insight, practical knowledge and knowhow. The reality is we have to speculate to accumulate and that is what Elaine is telling us to do. I feel like this book could come with a money back guarantee because if you follow it then you just can't fail to massively capitalise on selling your property.'

— **Zahra Pabani**, Partner, Irwin Mitchell LLP

'Staging is so important for property marketing these days. *Sell High, Sell Fast* gives you insight to all the tricks to help you sell your home faster. Working with Elaine and her team is fabulous, this book brings her expertise to the wider audience.'

— **Lee Armstrong**, Partner, Fine and Country

'Home staging has the power to completely transform a property, changing a prospective buyer's perception of how much they like the house. If nothing else, a room with furniture helps to provide scale and a better sense of space. This book is a step-by-step guide to why, when and how to achieve amazing results yourself or engage the services of a professional so that your sale stands the best possible chance of achieving the highest price in timely order. Great work!'

— **James Walker**, Director, Country Department, Savills (UK) Ltd

'This book is everything your estate agent wants you to know about how to present your property in order to get great photos and video before you sell. Read it, it works!'

— **Martyn Baum**, Director, Martyn Baum Consultancy and former President of the National Association of Estate Agents

SELL HIGH SELL FAST

How to sell your home for the best
possible price, in the quickest possible time

ELAINE PENHAUL

R3THINK PRESS

First published in Great Britain in 2020 by Rethink Press
(www.rethinkpress.com)

Cover image © Shutterstock | M.Leheda

Contents

Introduction

Sell High, Sell Fast asks questions of the way property is marketed in the UK. It compares the marketing strategies of other, much lower value products – such as cars and baked beans – to those applied to selling what is most people's biggest capital asset. I don't buy into the idea that buyers can, or should be expected to, see past clutter, dirt, dated decor and battered furnishings. I outline here the unique seven-step ADDRESS system used by my successful home staging company, Lemon and Lime Interiors. ADDRESS answers vendors' central question: 'How can I maximise the capital my home represents by selling it for as much money as quickly as possible?'

My aim in writing this book is to equip you, as a vendor, with the skills and knowledge to get your own home ready for sale. If you still feel that you don't have the time or the inclination to prepare your home yourself, then you'll understand how to engage a professional home stager and the services you can expect from them.

Home staging is not interior design, although the two are often confused. They're at opposite ends of a spectrum. Interior design is based around a homeowner's taste and living style. An interior designer will spend many hours understanding a family's needs before putting a scheme together. Home staging is interested only in creating market appeal for a property. It's a marketing tool and, as such, can be learned.

The way people approach buying property in the twenty-first century has changed dramatically. The way people sell property is changing much more slowly. There is often a disconnect between what a vendor is expecting to be able to sell and what a purchaser is willing to buy. This disconnect can lead to homes being stuck on the market for a long time without attracting an offer anywhere near what the vendor wants to achieve. While the evidence for this may be anecdotal, most agents will be able to tell stories about having two identical properties for sale on the same street. One is well cared for and beautifully presented and the other is more 'lived in'. The sale achieved on the well-maintained home, where the decor has been updated to reflect current trends and where clutter isn't on show, may attract an offer as much as 10% higher. The better-presented property sells almost immediately while the other languishes on the market for many months. A vendor who understands the psychology of their buyer and creates a property that is aspirational for their target buyer will be the one who achieves the highest offer in the shortest time.

This book sets the scene for understanding your market, finding your ideal buyer and creating a home with which they'll fall in love. My aim is to help you 'sell high, sell fast and move on'.

I have been fascinated by property my whole life. Even as a child I drove my mother mad by stopping to press my nose against the window of the local estate agent, Cruso and Wilkin, on the daily trip to the high street for groceries. I would go home and draw floor plans of houses.

Many years later, I divorced a property developer to whom I had been married for twenty years. As a result, I was thrown into a new role as director of a property management company in 2008. My career expertise at that time was in business coaching and teaching, not property. My degree is in maths, and post-university I had begun to train as an actuary. I wasn't well suited to an office-based career and ran away to spend a few years teaching sailing on a Greek beach in the early days of activity holidays in the Med. After returning, I taught maths in secondary school while I brought up my children. Over the years, I never lost my childhood fascination with property. I took apart two big country homes and rebuilt them during my marriage. It's the mix of property expertise and being mathematically minded, especially enjoying data collection, that gives me a unique edge in the property staging business. Most of our competitors come from a design background, and their focus is different. My team would argue I am much more interested in the numbers than the cushions. That is so true!

In a difficult period in my life, I had to decide whether to sell the property management business or learn how to maximise my opportunity by renting and selling my newly acquired portfolio to best advantage. With four small children to feed and a property market in global financial chaos, the decision wasn't hard, even though the learning has often been painful.

I set up Lemon and Lime Interiors in 2015 in an emerging UK home staging market. We have grown to be one of the biggest home staging companies in the UK, and we focus on the premium property market. I still love big country houses, even the ones so full of clutter it's hard to know where to start.

In this book, I explain what I've learned about the whys and hows of selling your home as quickly as you can for maximum financial gain. For most of us, selling a home represents far more than a simple bricks and mortar transaction. I know from experience the frustration in the limbo of not being able to sell and move on to the next stage of life. My ability to maximise my assets has been my route to a new, independent life and a career in an exciting area of property.

If you're selling, planning to sell or just want a new way to think about how you live in your own home, this is the book for you.

ONE

Marketing Property In The Twenty-First Century

How people shop is constantly evolving. This applies to purchasing a new home as well. Let's consider what has happened in the world of property marketing over the last thirty years. It's important to acknowledge how the internet, social media and online estate agency have significantly changed the way property is bought and sold. By the end of the chapter, you'll understand why you'll get your best sale if you attract offers quickly.

The chapters that follow explain how you can get your property marketing right – in other words, how you can sell your home for the best possible price in the shortest time.

The property market in the 2020s vs the 1990s

Since the mid-1990s, the internet has had a revolutionary effect on the way we communicate. It has changed the way we search for information, watch films and listen to music, and it has completely changed the way we shop. It has impacted our daily lives at home and at work. It's now difficult to imagine life without the access it gives us to our friends and families and our work, social and cultural lives. In the last few years, social media began dominating our communication and research.

The impact of the internet and social media has been as significant in the way we buy and sell our homes as it has in other areas of our lives. It has heralded the advent of the online estate agent and made it possible for even the most local agent to have a national presence by hosting their properties on internet portals such as Rightmove and Zoopla. In this chapter, my aim is to give some insight into how property marketing has changed and to highlight both the opportunities and the challenges offered by these changes when you decide to sell your home.

Then vs now

Estate agency in the nineties was local; a Rolodex or card box sat on agents' desks. There were no sophisticated 'matching' systems. Newspapers were the main source of advertising, with buyers from outside the area contacting a local paper and asking for a copy to be sent to them so they could do a property search in the area to which they wanted to move.

The usual way to sell a house in this period was to call a local agent, who would pop round, have a chat about the timing of the sale, take a few photos and create a brochure. The photos might sit on a board in the agent's window on the high street, and anyone looking for a new home would be able to go and have a look and discuss the property with the agent in the office. At the same time, the estate agent would usually have a list of anyone searching for a home in the area. When a newly listed property came to market, they would call the people on the list to get viewings in the diary.

In this way, the agent was a key factor in achieving both viewings and the sale. The relationship a vendor built with the agent was important. Vendor and agent spoke regularly to make sure they knew how much interest the property was getting. Mortgages were relatively easy to obtain, with many borrowers able to borrow up to six times their salary. In the eighties and the early nineties, the housing market was in a boom period. Property was seen as a sure thing in terms of investment, and owners expected the value to increase as a given. It was possible to make dramatic gains, and the baby boomer generation buying at that time expected their homes to be their investment plan and their pension.

And then, in 2008, came the global financial crash. Suddenly it was no longer possible for a prospective buyer to borrow money or get a mortgage easily. The banks and other lenders were cautious in a way that hadn't been seen before, and all confidence left the market. The notion of a home being a safe investment with a value that only increased over time became obsolete overnight. Far more people began to rent rather than buy, either because they couldn't borrow the money to buy or because they wanted to be cautious while things settled. In truth, the UK market has never fully settled since. For example, data from the Office for National Statistics says that the number of households in the private rented sector in the UK increased from 2.8 million in 2007 to 4.5 million in 2017.[1]

There are those who would argue that we are now in a much more realistic period about home ownership and that we have moved away from the 'boom and bust' approach to the housing market that dominated in the UK for many years. Conversely, many of the estate agents with whom I work feel that it has been harder to make a good living from agency, with good instructions harder to get to the market and more competition, including that from the rise of the online agent. The global economic crisis caused by the COVID-19 pandemic has influenced property prices too, with increases in prices in some parts of the market and

---

1   www.ons.gov.uk/economy/inflationandpriceindices/articles
     /ukprivaterentedsector/2018

significant drops in others, providing more evidence of how closely the housing market is tied in with political and economic uncertainty.

Things have changed. Let's take a quick look at all the ways that property is sold in 2020 that didn't exist in 1990.

Internet property portals

Rightmove started in 2000 and attracts around 150 million visits from home movers each month, with time spent on the site averaging 1.17 billion minutes per month.[2] In other words, people collectively spend over twenty years per month looking at properties on just one portal. This is a staggering statistic. It would be interesting to know how many of those views are by people looking to move imminently. The property portals have allowed a certain amount of voyeurism to creep into the property market; people will look to work out what their house might be worth by comparing it to what else is on the market. This is empowering to any homeowner who is planning to sell – they now have direct access to comparable data and can challenge an estate agent's valuation.

In 2020, there are three main internet portals serving the UK market – Rightmove, Zoopla and OnTheMarket.

---

2   www.rightmove.co.uk/press-centre/busiest-ever-month-on
     -rightmove-as-market-sees-confidence-return

com. Rightmove is the market leader, receiving **127.5 million visits per month**.[3] Zoopla says its websites (including Prime Location) and mobile apps attract over **50 million visits per month**.[4]

The 2016 *Which?* national home-moving survey asked 2,000 home buyers how they discovered the property they ended up buying. Over half (55%) had used traditional methods, such as looking in an estate agent's window or the local newspaper, while 45% had used more modern methods.[5] In 2020, social media took over as the way buyers find their home, with one premium agent reporting a 38% increase in traffic to their main website from social media between 2018 and 2019.[6]

Another big impact of technology's development has been the rise of the online agency.

Online vs high street agents

Online agency started around 2005. Purplebricks, the biggest of the online agents by approximately 60%,

---

3   www.hoa.org.uk/advice/guides-for-homeowners/i-am-selling
    /rightmove-zoopla-which-is-best/ www.thenegotiator.co.uk/portal
    -pressures
4   www.hoa.org.uk/advice/guides-for-homeowners/i-am-selling
    /rightmove-zoopla-which-is-best/ www.thenegotiator.co.uk/portal
    -pressures
5   www.which.co.uk/news/2016/09/only-four-in-10-find-new-homes
    -on-property-portals-451429
6   Fine and Country, Emilie Despois, 'Vision 2020 (Marketing)', Fine
    and Country Conference 2020, www.fineandcountry.com

started in 2012.[7] In the last quarter of 2019, according to *Which?* magazine, online agents, including Yopa, Tepilo and Emoov, had 7.9% of the market share.[8] It's difficult to predict whether this will grow. Online agency has suffered reputational damage in the recent past, but many agencies seem to be reinventing themselves and offering better service to their vendors. Arguably, the younger generation, who have grown up with technology as an integral part of their lives, prefer the anonymity of an online agent. Many people find them more convenient, as they're available at any time of day or night and, as a vendor, you have control.

They are certainly giving the traditional agents a challenge. All agents must now seriously consider what value they're bringing to the table. Charging higher fees isn't a problem if a vendor can clearly see what they're going to get for their money. There's always a place in any market for different levels of service with different fees. The Institute of Consumer Service says that 'despite economic pressures, the number of customers who prefer premium service, 27.6%, has remained consistent' (2018).[9] Many agents are cautious about charging high fees when vendors compare their service with online offerings. To some extent, this has

---

7 www.sellingup.com/purplebricks-online-estate-agent-timeline
8 www.which.co.uk/money/mortgages-and-property/home-movers
   /selling-a-house/online-estate-agents-ar2jr0g705uu
9 www.instituteofcustomerservice.com/research-insight/research
   -library/ukcsi-the-state-of-customer-satisfaction-in-the-uk-january
   -2018

led to what has been described as a 'race to the bottom', where the only way for an agent to feel as though they're in the running to gain an instruction is to slash a fee to under 1%. On average, UK agents charge the lowest fees to sell a home in the Western world.

The impact of social media

Many agents are turning to Facebook Marketplace as a viable selling tool. It doesn't yet seem to be an alternative to the property portals, but it's certainly an interesting development. One Midlands agent I spoke to, who habitually uses Facebook Marketplace for his marketing, said, 'Selling on Facebook is the next big disruptor in estate agency.'[10] The ability to actually sell a home through social media isn't yet the biggest impact of social media on the housing market. The bigger impact is how it influences the way people look for their new home. Explaining how platforms such as Instagram and Facebook have made a difference in the way people search for and view property is probably where I spend the most time during an initial consultation.

The iPad first came onto the market in 2010, Instagram launched later in the same year and WhatsApp appeared a few months before either. This technol-

---

10   With permission from Sean Newman of Fine and Country.

ogy infiltrated all aspects of our daily lives. We might imagine that when someone is actively looking for a new home, they're just looking at houses for sale. Historically this was the case – they couldn't see anything else in the window of an estate agent. Now, there are so many online platforms, as well as TV shows and magazines, that showcase beautiful homes. You only have to scroll through Instagram or Pinterest with an interior design hashtag for a few minutes to develop serious house envy. What this ability to scroll through endless images of houses creates is a dormant market. Dormant buyers are described by the estate agent industry as those people who weren't actively looking to move but, after falling in love with a property they saw while scrolling on their sofa, decided to sell their home.

The impact of photos and videos

Both the active and the dormant buyer offer opportunities that didn't exist ten years ago for a vendor. Statistics show that properties marketed through social media will achieve around six times more views than those marketed on just the online property portals.[11] As a vendor, knowing how much time your buyers are likely to spend looking at photos and videos online before they book to view is key. This understanding gives

---

11 Fine and Country, Emilie Despois, 'Vision 2020 (Marketing)', Fine and Country Conference 2020, www.fineandcountry.com

you a perfect chance to influence what they see as you launch your home onto the market.

Great presentation + professional photos =
your best sale

What exactly are potential buyers looking at? If you spend just fifteen minutes on any of the property portals, you'll quickly notice that not all properties in the same price bracket are equal in the way they're marketed. Presentation and photos are the important differences. I almost guarantee that you'll look at only three properties, in any price bracket you choose, before finding an unmade or badly-made bed. You'll look at even fewer properties to find decor you can date back to the year the property was bought, circa 1980. In nine out of ten properties you look at, it will appear as though the estate agent took the photos on their camera phone. If one of these is your house, most of your potential buyers will move on to the next set of photos, the equivalent of 'swiping left' on a dating site.

The global pandemic (COVID-19) is driving another shift in marketing. Those homes which didn't have a video or virtual tour option as the country went into lockdown were at a distinct disadvantage at a time when there were more people than ever with time on their hands, viewing properties online. As the world moves into a 'new normal' with social distancing commonplace for some time, the number of physical viewings at an occupied property will likely be reduced. Videos and virtual tours will become an essential part of a marketing pack.

Creating the win-win-win

Selling a home is a partnership – and in any partnership, every stakeholder needs to feel they're getting the best deal possible. Thinking about the sale of your home in this way will help you think through what you're bringing to the market. If you can get into the headspace of your agent and your buyer, you're going to get the best deal for yourself as the vendor too.

If you're selling, you're likely also planning to buy, so you have a head start in this process. Use your own mindset as you think about your future home to inform what you imagine the buyer of your property might be thinking. They may be looking for a different type of property to the one you're now searching for. Consider which stage you're in as a buyer and who the person buying your home will be. Will they be a first-time buyer, a young family or perhaps someone downsizing? Both you and your buyer will be looking for a home to move into and to get the maximum value for your funds. You can understand from your own perspective that your buyer needs to believe that the property they buy offers the best value on the market in the area where they're looking. Buying a home is both a head and a heart decision for most people. Ensuring your property stacks up from both perspectives will quickly put you ahead of the game.

Your buyer is probably looking online to find a house to fall in love with. They will also want to know that it ticks most of their logical criteria – price, location and so on. Some people looking at a move may be considering buying the worst house on the best street they can afford, but this breed of buyer is much less common in the 2020s than it was even ten years ago. Once someone has decided to view, you must encourage them to make the emotional decision to buy from the moment they walk through the door. Your main aim as the vendor is to make your potential buyer feel as though your home is the only one for them. At the same time, from a logical viewpoint, they need to feel they're getting a great deal.

The second person in the win-win-win partnership is your chosen estate agent. What motivates agents is an interesting question. It's worth spending a little time thinking about how they operate. You might want to consider whether your agent is employed or self-employed. Are they paid on a pure salary or part-commission basis, or are they running their own business? A self-employed business owner or an agent paid mainly on a commission basis will probably be motivated to see results from your sale sooner than someone who is salaried. They will all, to a greater or lesser extent, be motivated by money, reputation or both. What does your agent need to achieve so that they feel as though taking the instruction for your sale is worth their time and effort? In a post-COVID-19 world, it may be that many agents are anxious to take on any instruction to get business moving again. But be careful – there will also be agencies who can no longer afford to operate, and you don't want to be the vendor working with an agent who charges a low fee to get new instructions and then goes out of business part way through your sale.

The time an agent puts in to visiting your home, researching other properties in the area to get the right valuation, preparing marketing material and conducting viewings is significant. Your agent may also be helping to progress your sale, chasing solicitors and acting as the point of contact between you and your buyer. A house which takes a long time to sell doesn't represent a win for the agent on any level, and their motivation will drop once the sale starts to feel too hard through no fault of their own.

Finally, the third partner in the deal is you, as the vendor. You want to achieve the maximum value for your property with the minimum waiting time and effort on your part. Being on the market for a long time is exhausting, not least because you have to tidy up before every viewing. Perhaps you've lived in your home for a long time and it will be a wrench to leave. Perhaps you're excited about moving on to a new adventure and don't want to feel in limbo for too long. You may have invested significant time, money and effort in improving your home since you bought it and need to see that investment rewarded. In any case, your home is likely to be your biggest capital asset and your passport to the next stage of your life. You absolutely need to win the game of beating the competition to the best buyer out there.

Why is selling fast so important?

When I was a student, a friend who was studying marketing tried to explain the economic theory of supply and demand to me. Then, it seemed counter-intuitive that as demand for a product increases, so would price increase. Many years and a lot of observation later, I've come to accept that this is a true reflection of how we buy. A good example of this is flights. As flights become more popular online and the number of people searching and looking for one particular flight increases, the cost of the flight goes up.

A product will be bought at its highest price quickly, if it's desirable. Any product which is less desirable will take longer to sell and will eventually be bought at a lower price point. This has been evident in the property market for many years. The longer a property remains on the market with no buyer, the more the price will be decreased to try to attract interest. The properties which are snapped up quickly tend to be sold at, or even over, their original guide price. They are the 'hot properties'. The agents of these properties have done a good job getting both the valuation and the marketing right from the outset and creating a buzz which draws in multiple buyers. In some cases, this starts a bidding war and pushes the offer that is accepted higher than the guide price. Great news if you're the vendor. This is generally a much more effective way of achieving a great sale than the more usual British approach, which has people saying to their agent, 'Well let's try it at the highest value we can possibly justify. We're not in a hurry so we can wait for the right buyer to come along.' From a logical and economic perspective, this approach is destined to fail. It will, more often than not, lead to frustration for all concerned. But it's still the way many vendors, and agents, will approach the market.

Other factors will influence the need for a fast sale. Charlie Sylvanus-Jones, a Leicestershire estate agent, says, 'The digital era and tech such as smartphones have reduced the "shelf-life" of properties from an olde-worlde norm of 12 weeks to approximately 30 days.'[12]

He makes the point that the rise in the use of technology means that people generally have shorter attention spans. This impacts how we sell our homes. When everything we need in everyday life is accessible through a button on our phone, it's hard to wait for something to happen. I remember watching a television

---

12   With permission from Charlie Sylvanus-Jones.

series that aired on Monday nights and the frustration of having to be patient until the following week to see what happened. Now we can watch anything we want at a time that suits us. Many series are released in full on iPlayer or Netflix the moment the first episode is shown on terrestrial TV. Because of our instant culture, buyers will notice if a property has been online for more than a few weeks, and it will no longer attract the click-throughs – it will have gone stale. Many buyers will believe that it's still online because there's something wrong with it.

You may have more personal reasons why a quick sale is important. Your sale may be driven by a relocation, for example. We have worked with families where one partner has been relocated for work. The other partner stays with the house that's on the market, not wishing to leave it empty, vulnerable to crime or damage. Empty houses are hard to insure. Insurers, understandably, require assurance that the house is being visited regularly to identify any potential harm – for example, a burst pipe causing major water damage during the winter months, tile slippage in high winds leading to water ingress through the roof and so on. Empty properties are notoriously hard to sell in the UK, especially if they have been closed up due to a relocation and aren't being aired regularly. Our climate quickly leads to a musty, damp smell which is unattractive to buyers.

Family tragedy brings property to the market and will usually necessitate a quick sale. If a property is part of the estate of a deceased person, there will be probate costs and taxes to pay. Until the property is sold, none of the capital can be released to the beneficiaries and cash flow is halted. Perhaps divorce or separation is the motivation for a sale. Living in a home which is a disputed joint asset is never comfortable – I know, I've been there! A quick sale in all these instances is a gateway to establishing a new trajectory in life. Releasing the capital asset held in the house is so important.

We see an increasing number of sales as a result of people wanting to downsize and release some of the capital in the house to travel and to fund an active retirement. In some cases, parents want to help their children onto the property ladder and use the sale of the family home to do so.

There are many and varied reasons why selling fast is so important, both economically and psychologically. You can drive a considered approach to marketing your property by working closely with your agent and being realistic about what you're trying to achieve. Your perfect sale will reach the highest possible price in the fastest possible time.

The good news is that, as a vendor, now you're beginning to build a picture of how the market has changed, perhaps out of all recognition, since you bought your home.

In summary

- Selling fast is the best way to attract the highest offers. The longer your property sits on the market, the less likely you are to achieve your ideal price; you'll be held in the limbo land of 'unsold', unable to move on to the next stage of your life.

- Create the win-win-win situation for vendor-agent-buyer for your best sale.

It's time to do some myth-busting and learn tips from our experience of working with vendors to achieve their best sales.

TWO

The Importance Of Presentation

Buyers decide quickly if they are interested in buying a home, perhaps even within the first ten seconds or so. These days, those precious first seconds are spent looking at your photos online. These comprise your shop window for prospective buyers, your chance to catch their attention. They need to be the best you can possibly achieve. Hiring a professional photographer and a videographer is one step, but the best photographer in the world can photograph only what's in front of them. Achieving the perfect photos will depend a lot on the work you do before they arrive with a camera.

The rise of home staging

In 1999, in the USA, Barb Schwarz founded the first industry trade association focused purely on getting homes ready for sale: the International Association of Home Staging Professionals, IAHSP®. She describes home staging as 'a tool for communication'.[13]

I use the term 'home staging' throughout the book. For several years, I was reluctant to use it, preferring 'professional property presentation'. Now, estate agencies in the UK, and homeowners as a result, have become more used to 'home staging'. We're moving away from the idea of it being an American fad and accepting that it's a key part of marketing a home.

In essence, 'home staging' means 'preparing a home for sale'. The goal of staging is to make a home appealing to the highest number of potential buyers, helping it to sell more swiftly and for more money. Staging techniques focus on improving a property's appeal by transforming it into a welcoming, attractive product that anyone might want. In staging your home, you're aiming to communicate the lifestyle it offers to a buyer. As mentioned, buying a home is a joint decision between the head and the heart. Staging is your tool to capture the heart.

When I started my business in 2015, CNN had placed home staging on the list of the top seven fastest growing industries in the USA.[14] A similar phenomenon

---

13 www.barbschwarz.com
14 www.edition.cnn.com/2009/LIVING/worklife/08/04/cb.7.emerging
    .jobs

has happened in many other countries, including much of Europe. Sanja Radovic of IAHSP®Europe (the European branch of IAHSP) says,

> 'More and more RE professionals, as well as homeowners, are aware of the benefits and profits that Home Staging adds to the RE transactions. Information and education are the keys to make our profession widely known. IAHSP® EU will continue to focus on building the well-deserved credibility and bringing recognition to our profession in Europe. One day, hopefully very soon, Home Staging will become a blooming industry in Europe too.'[15]

Home staging vs interior design

One of the misconceptions we've struggled with as a business has been the equating of home staging with interior design. I continue to work hard to dispel this myth. Home staging is a property marketing tool. Usually it doesn't take into account the tastes or wishes of the property's owner. The design of the rooms is predicated on what the agent and the stager working together believe will attract the widest target audience for a property of its type.

---

15   Sanja Radovic, International Association of Home Staging Professionals, phone interview, 21 January 2020

Interior design is an art form which aims to make a room more aesthetically pleasing to the people living in it. When we home stage a property, we don't know who is going to be living there. We make an educated guess and use research to discover what this target group might want to see in their new home. We follow market trends, but we don't buy furniture that is overtly fashionable. Most furniture used for staging is rented into one property after another and may need to look current for several years. I have detailed how renting furniture works in practical terms for a vendor in Chapter Seven.

What is the benefit of home staging?

Vendors and agents have had to work harder post-2008 to attract good buyers. A number of factors have slowed down the market over the last few years, including the uncertainty of Brexit and COVID-19 – the latter brought the housing market, along with everything else, to a dramatic halt. The UK has been relatively slow to understand and embrace staging as a legitimate property marketing tool, seeing it at least in part as a dishonest representation of reality. This I find interesting. As a society, we are happy to accept that everything else we might want to buy is advertised and sold to us through great photos, videography, TV and the internet. And yet, often when we see a home that has been well-dressed in preparation for being sold, we Brits are suspicious. We worry that maybe the vendor is trying to hide something behind beautiful furniture and decor. We seem to have a strange relationship with property and a deep distrust of anyone selling homes.

Home staging professionals don't use staging to create a false reality but to show off a home at its best. This is no different from putting on our best clothes for an important interview. Most people would love to live in a home which is immaculate and tidy, to have a kitchen that looks like a page from a glossy interiors magazine and to fall into a bed worthy of a five-star hotel. But most of us know that once we've bought a house and moved in, it's unlikely that the house will ever look so tidy again. While we're searching for a new home, we love to be under the illusion of an idealised world. This is where staging becomes so important.

Ultimately, selling your home is you pitching what you have to offer against the competition. Your aim is to attract the buyer ready to move and to ensure it's your home they fall in love with. You want to move on to the next stage of your life, whatever that holds for you. You don't want to be held up in a world where you have to tidy up every few days and entertain strangers asking crazy questions in your kitchen. Launch your home to the market with a bang not a whimper, looking as though you actually want to sell, not as though you're just testing the market. Now we come to the 'how'.

ADDRESS your marketing if you want to change your ADDRESS!

Our unique ADDRESS system to Sell High, Sell Fast

Getting ready to sell can be a lengthy process – don't underestimate the preparation time. My first blog after starting the business talked about preparing for the sale at least a month before calling an agent for a valuation. These days, with more experience, I advise starting a good three months in advance or more, depending on the house's value and how long you've lived in it. If you were planning a big party or a family wedding, you'd think nothing of making lists and starting the organising months, or even years, in advance. Moving house is at least as big an event in most people's lives as a wedding or a big party, yet we don't imagine it's something we need to physically prepare for in the same way. If this sounds daunting, don't worry. There's a growing industry of professional home stagers who can help throughout the process.

Another reason to start early is to have time to be kind to yourself. Houses are emotional places. Don't rush your preparation or you'll find yourself feeling frazzled and stressed, unable to decide what to do first. The moving process is mired in difficult decisions about personal belongings and may cause memories to surface that halt progress for a while. Don't worry. Keep your end goal – your new home and the next stage of your life – in mind as you begin. There is help available should you need it: you can call a friend, a family member or a professional stager. At Lemon and Lime Interiors, we recruit our staff as much on their emotional intelligence as on their ability to arrange cushions. We know teaching our team to tidy and position furniture and accessories to best effect is a relatively straightforward process. What's equally important is their ability to read a situation and understand when it's time to pause, put the kettle on and chat.

A LITTLE COMPASSION GOES A LONG WAY

One day my team called from the property they were dressing and asked if I knew why the vendor, Jules, had been sitting in a chair all day just watching them work. They had included her in conversations and made tea at regular intervals so that she would be part of the team. But they were worried they were missing a crucial instruction or piece of information which would explain her behaviour. I said I had no idea but to carry on what they were doing and keep chatting. The next day, Jules sent me a lovely email. She said she hoped the ladies didn't mind that she had been watching them all day – she had suddenly felt overwhelmed with grief. For her, the day the dated furniture was removed and the new was installed to attract a buyer was the day her mother really left the house, even though her mother had died several months earlier. The kindness my team had showed in not asking intrusive questions or requesting that she leave them to their work without watching was something she really valued and made a difficult day a little bit easier.

I imagine that all types of vendors will be reading this book. Some of you will need to start right at the beginning of the process and others will have already either made a start or perhaps done a build or renovation project and won't need tips on decluttering or decorating. You might want to skip to the 'R' or even the 'E' stage of the process, though I'd advise skimming through the earlier stages to make sure you haven't missed any tips. The next chapters contain many details and stories, but I have summarised them here too, so if you're the type of person who just needs the instructions, you're good to go at the end of this chapter.

So, what is the ADDRESS system? Put simply, it's a set of sequential steps that will move you from feeling overwhelmed to feeling in control and proud that you have such a beautiful home to show your viewers. Crucially, this beautiful home is probably the major asset that will release the capital you need to move into the next stage of your life.

The seven steps to ADDRESS

- Assess

- Declutter

- Decorate

- Re-imagine

- Emphasise

- Stage
- Sell

We'll look at each in more detail in this chapter. The following chapters will expand on the ideas to help you feel ready to make a start with your own home. Or you'll recognise the value in taking the steps but see that you need some help.

Assess

First, and crucially, you need to work out who your ideal buyer is and assess what your home is offering them. It's important to do a little homework to assess the competition in your neighbourhood and compare what you have to offer against the other houses your buyer will be viewing. The next step is to decide how much work you must do on your home before you have any marketing photos or videos done. The sense of panic this step instils in many of our vendors is perfectly understandable – this is your 'lived-in' home. But stay calm. I'm often asked, 'Is my home worse than anything else you've seen?' Trust me, you would have to be in a real mess for that to be the case. Occasionally I've had to drive straight home to shower after visiting a home before heading back to the office. Thank goodness this is rare!

In this step:

- Why are you selling?
- Who is your buyer?

- What else is on the market that your buyers are going to be looking at?

- Take photos of your home.

- Create a mood board of what you like in the homes you view.

- How much clutter do you have?

- Ask a friend if your home has an unpleasant smell.

- Take a good look at your garden and any outbuildings and assess those too.

- Examine your exterior decoration to ensure your buyer doesn't just drive past.

- Does your internal decor appear tired or dated?

- Look closely at your carpets – do they need cleaning or replacing?

- Write a to-do list and recruit help if you're feeling overwhelmed.

Declutter

This is usually the hardest stage and must be done before decorating or restyling your rooms. If you commission a decorator to paint your walls to freshen them up, they will charge you considerably more if they have to move everything around to get past your clutter. It makes financial sense to give your decorator the best chance to reach what they need to without falling over the mess.

In this step:

- Equip yourself with boxes, labels and marker pens.
- Decide what is to stay and what must go.
- Allocate everything into piles – 'keep out', 'keep but pack now', 'throw away'.
- Get the 'throw away' pile out of the house and off to its final home.
- Decide whether you have space at home to store your 'keep but pack now' pile or whether you need to find storage off-site.
- Clean.

Decorate

Now is the time to get the decorator in to paint those walls a neutral colour. See Chapter Five for top tips on colour. White isn't necessarily white, and just because grey is fashionable, it doesn't mean it's the right neutral for your home.

In this step:

- Find a decorator who can come quickly – it's worth paying a little more to get on the market sooner.
- Take advice on the best colours to attract a buyer. It's something that daunts many vendors (again, see Chapter Five; I'll talk you through it).

- Look at your ceilings and woodwork as well as the walls. They may also need doing.

- Painting one room may make other rooms look tired, so be prepared to do a bit more than you'd planned.

- Don't forget the external woodwork (fascia boards and windows) and especially the garden gates.

- Complete any minor repairs at this stage.

Re-imagine

You live in your home in the way that suits you. This may or may not make sense to other people. Stand back and remember how the rooms evolved. Compare your family's set-up to that of your anticipated buyer. Then re-imagine how the rooms might be used in a different way by another family. Do these ways make more sense? Could you change the rooms ahead of your sale?

In this step:

- Be objective in your assessment of why each room is used for its current purpose. Some home stagers may offer feedback on this as part of a free initial consultation.

- Does each room have a clearly defined function?

- Is the function of each room one which has relevance to most of the buyers you believe will be interested in buying your home?

- If not, you need to rearrange your furniture or rent furniture that will define the function more clearly.

- Check that the flow of your home makes sense. Make sure the way each room links with its neighbouring rooms will be appealing to a broad range of people. Now is the time to change things if necessary.

Emphasise

This is the moment where you decide which lifestyle aspects of your home you want to draw your buyer's attention to. You'll cleverly emphasise your home's best features and endeavour to draw focus away from anything that is less than ideal.

In this step:

- Identify the areas you think are the strongest features of your home – perhaps an amazing conservatory, a cosy window seat, a contemporary kitchen or a sumptuous bathroom.

- How do you use these areas?

- What do you love about them?

- What can you do to tell the story of these areas to your viewers?

- Make a list of what needs to be done and what props you might need to really show off the spaces.

Stage

Staging is the bit where you bring everything together and put all your props, additional furniture and accessories into place. By the time you get here, you will have decided where you need additional furniture or whether you'll need to furnish the whole house. If you've moved out already, you may be looking to furnish everything. If you're still living in your home, you may be adding soft furnishings, accessories and perhaps replacing tired furniture to attract your target buyer.

In this step:

- Get everything together that you're going to need. Choose a staging company to work with if you want a lot of additional items. It will probably be much more cost-effective to rent than buy.

- If you're staging your own home using the things you have, think about the focal point of each room and about using symmetry and creating balance for maximum effect.

- You may want to seek help positioning everything and creating the perfect scenarios in your home. Professional staging companies will do this for you, or you may have a friend with a great eye.

- If you're bringing in new furniture, make sure the staging company provides a bespoke solution tailored for your home, not a furniture package.

- Book the photographer to come immediately after the staging is finished so there's no chance of messing things up. Go out for dinner or even to a hotel for the night ahead of the photos being done. You may need to keep the kids and any pets out of the way for the evening too.

Sell

Now that you've done all your preparation, it's time to mobilise your team into action, although some of them may have been involved from the outset. Ensure everything is ready so that when you have agreed on an offer, the sale can progress quickly and you can move on to the next exciting chapter in your life. At this stage, you're probably looking for your new home too. Having everything in place early will really help move things along once you accept an offer.

In this step:

- Make sure you've signed all the paperwork your agent has given you.

- Approve your brochure and your online marketing as soon as the photos come back from the photographer. Do make sure your agent is using a professional photographer – no point spending a lot of time and effort getting your home looking great if the photography doesn't show it at its best.

- Check in with your agent at least once a week. Be proactive – don't leave it to your agent to call you.

- Ensure you, or your agent, have collated all the documents and information a viewer is likely to ask for.

- Choose a solicitor and let them know you're selling ahead of any offers coming in. If you instruct them early, they'll get your property pack ready with all the necessary forms. This way, everything will be available as soon as you have accepted an offer.

- Keep in touch with your solicitor once you have accepted an offer. Understand exactly what stage the progression of your sale is in and where any hold-ups occur so that you can act quickly to move things along if necessary.

- Start planning your move, whether you have bought or you're moving into rented accommodation.

In summary

- Buyers look online for property first. Your photos are your shop window.

- Even the best professional photographer can photograph only what is in front of them. If you don't care about the presentation of your home, don't expect the photographer to wave a magic wand.

- Buyers are also looking at property photos of fully interior designed and professionally photographed homes on social media. The bar they're comparing the photos of your home against is high.

- Home staging is a property marketing tool and aims to make a home appealing to a wide target market. It is not the same as interior design which, usually, strives to make a home appealing for the home owner.

Use a systemised approach to prepare for your sale to make sure you have everything covered. We use ADDRESS – assess, declutter, decorate, re-imagine, emphasise, stage and sell.

THREE

Assess

This is the first step in our ADDRESS system. Assess is the planning stage. There are three aspects to get right before you move on to the decluttering, decorating, etc. that you were probably expecting to have to do when you picked up this book. Firstly, it's important to know why you're selling. Secondly, you need to figure out who you believe your buyer will be. Finally, you must take a good look at your home and assess how what you're selling compares with what you think your buyer will be looking for. As is the case for most big events, if you spend time in the planning stage, things will go more smoothly.

Why are you selling?

There are many reasons why people sell, including:

- Job relocation
- Divorce
- Marriage/moving in with a partner
- Downsizing
- Upsizing
- Investment purposes
- Death
- A change is fancied

Of the properties my business has been involved with in the last four years, and not including the new builds, about 80% of the sales fall into one of the 'D' categories: death, divorce or downsizing. Not many people are upsizing – they have already reached the point of living in their 'forever home' or what they believed, at the time of buying, to be their 'forever home'.

'Forever home' is a bit of a misnomer. It's hard to be sure that anything you purchase is forever, whether it's a handbag or a house. Life circumstances change and, with them, the need for property. When it comes to your sale, and to the purchase being made by your buyer, there will likely be many emotional decisions being made alongside the more logical ones.

Buying or selling a house is the biggest financial transaction most people will ever make. If you were buying or selling as an investor, you'd find a lot of advice, training courses and coaching available. But as a domestic home owner, you'll find little available to you. You want the best investment for your money. You also want to know that you'll be happy in the home you choose – one that's in the right location, with the best schools and the best Wi-Fi. You'll likely have so many questions as a buyer. You can leverage this emotional need of your potential buyers in your position as a seller to achieve that win-win-win you're looking for.

What can you offer your buyer? You, or your agent, could prepare a presentation that lists the things you love about living in your house. Some agents work with owners to create a testimonial. Increasingly, as a response to the impact on house viewings during COVID-19, these are appearing in video format too. As a potential buyer, being handed a list of answers to all the questions you might think of as soon as you leave a viewing may well make you more likely to buy. A note of caution though: try to strike a happy balance between being informative and being overly pushy.

Your reason for selling may determine the price you're prepared to accept. For example, in a situation where a property is being sold due to a divorce or separation, both partners will want to be able to buy something new following the sale. In many cases, understandably, neither party wants to compromise on space in their new home. They understand that they will have only half the capital each to invest in a new home, but they still don't want to significantly downsize. This is especially true if they have children to consider. In this situation, maximising the financial gain from the family home is critical. Properties being sold as the result of a divorce are often easy to spot from photos. Perhaps one partner has moved out already and taken pictures or furniture with them. The photos on the property portals may show spaces on the walls where the paint has faded.

GETTING CREATIVE

I once went to see a property for sale as a result of divorce and the partner who had left had taken half of everything. She'd left with one bedside table of every pair, three of the set of six dining chairs and one sofa of the pair in the sitting room. It was apparent as soon as anyone walked into that house that there was a pretty acrimonious separation happening.

Our challenge was to make the house look normal again without huge cost. Fortunately, mismatched dining chairs are fashionable and we kept the style of the chairs similar but used alternating colours. Armchairs easily replaced the missing sofa, but we did have to start again with the bedside tables. Not even our expertise could make the odd bedsides look attractive.

When it's clear that a house is being sold because of a divorce, the impact is threefold. Firstly, the buyer might be put off of making an offer because they believe, usually rightly, that the sale won't go through smoothly because of the tug of war happening between the divorcing partners. Secondly, the house doesn't feel happy and most people don't want to buy an unhappy house. And thirdly, it looks as though the vendor just wants to get out of the situation. This being the case, a potential buyer may well make a cheeky offer in the hope that the vendor will accept so they can move on with their life quickly.

If you're the vendor in this situation, you may not be able to accept a low offer. It could be that you're desperate to move on but need to achieve the highest possible value for the house so that both you and your ex can buy something else. If you have young children, you may need to minimise the impact of the change on them and ensure both houses have separate rooms for them. This is one of the situations where good advice about how to prepare before you sell is crucial.

A property coming on to the market as part of an estate of someone who has died is another interesting, and common, case in our world. Several siblings may be left with the responsibility of selling their parents' home. It may be that there has been a period of ill health and so the functionality of the rooms has changed – a bedroom has moved downstairs, for instance. It may be that the parent was living in a care home or with another family member for a while and the house has been left unoccupied or even tenanted. Inevitably, the house will have dated decor, patterned carpets, old-fashioned furniture and, in some cases, so much clutter it's hard to see the walls and floors at all. The tidying and sorting of all this 'stuff' is difficult to do after a bereavement, especially in the situation where the beneficiaries of the estate aren't local and must travel long distances on a weekend to sort the house.

These types of sales, even at the top of the market, are easy to identify on the internet. The work on the presentation has only been partially done, the approach being, 'Well, someone will see past all this and want to put their own stamp on it anyway'. As soon as a viewer walks into the house, the smell of spills on the carpet, lingering disinfectant and worse is unmistakable. Immediately an experienced buyer will be thinking, 'I bet the family just wants to get rid of this one as quickly as they can.' This may mean that the offers are much lower than the asking price. Alternatively, if the house is a neglected one in an excellent area, buyers could be falling over themselves to put in offers. The key here is for you, as the vendor, to capitalise on the interest by presenting the house in the best light possible.

Who is your buyer?

One of the most important exercises we ask vendors to do is work out who they believe their buyer will be. Some agents are really helpful at this stage. It's worth seeking out one who has good experience of the local market. The best agents will know who's already looking in the area for a property like yours. They will understand whether the area is currently appealing to families with young children; it may be that the local school has been rated 'outstanding' during a recent Ofsted inspection. They'll also know whether it's an area appealing to downsizers. You may be able to work this out for yourself – walking down your local high street will give you an idea. People-watching is a great pastime and especially useful when you're selling your home. It's worth putting aside any preconceptions you may have about your area. Often vendors believe the people in their neighbourhood are people like them (a reflection of their social circle). It can be eye opening to sit at a table in the window of the high street café and drink coffee watching passers-by for a while. Notice the cars parked along the street. This is a good gauge of the area's affluence.

The intergenerational sale

One of the problems we encounter almost daily is the different approach different generations have to property purchase. The approach to buying also dictates expectations around selling. Millennials and Generation Z now make up more than half the population of the world (Deloitte Millennial Survey 2019).[16] But property ownership, especially at the higher end of the market, is still primarily in the hands of the baby boomers and early Generation X.

---

16   www2.deloitte.com/content/dam/Deloitte/global/Documents
     /About-Deloitte/deloitte-2019-millennial-survey.pdf

Baby boomers bought at a time when property was relatively affordable in comparison to salary. On top of that, they were the generation brought up by post-war parents with a DIY and 'make do and mend' approach to life. Their family home might have been bought as a project house – something they could see would be beautiful given a lot of time, effort and hard work. This generation, especially outside London, owns many of the country homes which have been renovated in the last forty years.

Millennials have an entirely different approach to life. This generation expects instant solutions. They have grown up with answers, in the form of the internet, at their fingertips. So when they buy property, to a large extent they expect to be buying an instant solution. It may be a project to flip, in which case they need to buy cheaply – the goal they're after is instant profit. More likely they're looking for an instant home to invite friends round to see. This generation value experiences. They aspire to travel and to help more in their communities. Their home purchase, spending hard-earned cash and committing to a huge mortgage, needs to represent an amazing life experience too, somewhere they can have fun with their friends and show off as the result of their great job. They certainly don't want to view properties which look as though they'll require not only more cash to be sunk into them but also time and energy they simply don't have.

Once you have a realistic and current understanding of the general demographic, assess your home and make a list. Is it a four-bedroom family home? Do you have a large open-plan living/kitchen area? If so, you're probably going to attract a family. If all the bedrooms are on the same level, most families will look; if the bedrooms are on different levels, it will appeal to a family with older children. The features of the local area you want to advertise may differ accordingly.

Three-bedroom properties are interesting – they can be equally attractive to a family upsizing or a couple downsizing. Large country properties with land and six bedrooms have a specific market. This is where an agent who understands this type of property and the buyer you're seeking is vital.

A property which has a small kitchen separate from the living space is difficult to sell in the current market. For some time, open-plan living has been in style, and while the desire for separate reception rooms certainly hasn't disappeared, and in some cases is trending again, rarely do buyers want a small galley-style kitchen with no eating area. You may not want to take a wall down to open up the kitchen into the living area ahead of your sale, although this could pay dividends. The way around the problem might be to ask an architect or even a builder to draw plans that show the area opened up and provide some idea of costs for doing the work. This can help your viewers get the picture and realise that it probably won't be as costly to do as they might fear.

Good Wi-Fi is crucial for most buying groups these days, and it's easy for someone to look up internet speeds in your area. If this is a problem, you may need to upgrade your service before selling.

Let's consider in more detail what different buyer types may be looking for.

Family with young children – These people will want good primary schools within walking distance, perhaps something on a bus route for a good secondary school too. They'll also be looking for bedrooms all on the same level, an open-plan living space, a home that's in walking distance to local amenities, shops, etc. and a garden which offers 'playing space'.

Family with older children still at school – These buyers will also want good secondary schools within walking distance or on a bus route. They might look for open-plan living space and a room separate from the family living space which can be used as a TV room, study or snug. The bedrooms don't necessarily need to be on the same level, but these buyers may look for at least one bathroom on each level. They might also want to see plenty of off-road parking.

Empty nesters – They may want a home with an annex or attic rooms that can be used for children who bounce back post-university or who are saving for their first home. These buyers are often the 'sandwich generation' – if they don't need space for adult offspring, they may need space for elderly parents. These people will often have bought at a time when it was more common to take on a project and probably won't be afraid to redecorate if necessary. They will expect to have entertaining space and love open-plan rooms or rooms which can be opened to the garden.

Downsizers – If they're still relatively young and in good health, they may be empty nesters. Equally, they may be downsizing so that they can travel and be looking for a 'lock-up and leave' property. In this case, they'll want something which is in good order and doesn't need any work.

We see many people who are still relatively young, in their fifties or early sixties, downsizing. They're still fit and healthy and are choosing to plan well ahead. These people look for a home which has adaptable space – perhaps a ground-floor annex they can use as their main home at some point or rooms that could be converted to ground-floor living later and an upstairs that might be used as a flat for other family.

Having established who your target buyer is likely to be, now it's time to get started on the practicalities.

How much work needs to be done?

This is the million-dollar question. It's hard to be objective about your own home, and the longer you've lived there, the harder it will be. You may need to enlist the help of friends and family members. Don't ask the ones who will always say, 'But your home is lovely, it's so comfortable. You don't need to do anything.' This is great affirmation on a day when you feel as though everywhere is a tip, you have friends coming for dinner and no time to push the Hoover around. It isn't helpful when it comes to assessing your home before selling. You need the friend who will be honest with you and, preferably, will offer to help you achieve what needs to be done! If you don't think you'll get this from anyone in your close circle, it may be time to recruit professional help – it will definitely pay off. In Chapter Nine, I discuss how to find the right professionals for your team.

Start by becoming your own potential buyer and notice what you see. The next chapters will explain what to look for as you walk through your home. Equip yourself with a notebook and a camera. Take photos as you walk around. When I sit down at my desk to review my notes and photos after seeing a house for the first time, I often notice things in the photos that I didn't see during the walk. Remember that your agent will be putting photos of most rooms in your house online before you get anyone coming to view. The camera may well pick up features that aren't as noticeable when you're standing in a room, especially when it's one with which you're already familiar. Take photos from each corner of a room and then look at them critically on a computer screen – you'll be surprised by what you notice! Some property staging companies, including ours, offer a service which looks at your photos and comments on what you could do to improve the subject matter rather than the photo quality.

Notice what you notice when you view to buy. As discussed, it's likely that if you're selling, you're also looking to buy. You'll be scrolling through lots of photos online, and perhaps you've already been on viewings. Use this as an opportunity to inform how you need to sell. What do you notice when you look at the homes you're viewing? Is it the lovely space and light they offer, or are you finding it tricky to see past clutter and dirty carpets? It's well worth creating a profile of an aspirational home. Use Pinterest or a similar app to capture photos that you see online and like, or make a list of links to homes you love – not homes you're able to buy, necessarily, but ones to which you're instantly attracted.

It's difficult to detach yourself emotionally from your home and see it as viewers will see it. But if you possibly can, try to relate what you're seeing as aspirational homes to what you're offering in selling your home. What will your buyer be looking for in the house they buy? The competition is tough. You need to be selling the great things about your home and the lifestyle it can afford.

Once you've completed all aspects of the assessment step, it's time to make a list. This list will determine a time frame for getting your home onto the market. How much work needs to be done to make your home the best in the price bracket in your area? This may include decorating and external work. It may include minor repairs which have been neglected for a long time or have gone unnoticed. You may simply need to do a little tidying and a good clean. This is also the best time to decide how much help you need. Which trades are necessary? Decorators, plumbers, electricians or a handyman or handywoman? All these people are likely to be busy, so the earlier you can book them in, the better. This is a good reason for starting to assess your home at least six months ahead of wanting to sell, if possible.

Assess outside too

Start by driving up to your house – and I do mean get into the car, drive around the block and come back, approaching from the direction you think your viewers are most likely to come from. As you stop, take a moment or two and really look at the first impression your viewers will get. Look at the garden, the drive, the front of the house. You're looking for anything that makes you think 'wow!' in either a good way or a bad way. Identify the 'wow' and analyse it. Is it directed at a feature you need to enhance – something that will attract a buyer before they've even got inside? Or is it work that needs to be done ahead of calling the estate agent?

Things to consider:

- Is it easy to identify the house, either by its name or a number? The number should be visible from the road, not just as you approach the door. It's easy to make a potential buyer cross before they've even arrived by keeping the location of the house a secret (no signage or dirty or broken plaques).

- Make sure the front door is clearly identifiable and the route to get there is obvious. One house we did was two cottages that had been knocked into one. The house still had two front gates and two doors, and it was impossible from the outside to tell which entrance was the one the owners used. Once we solved this problem, the house sold quickly.

- Tidy the front garden, clear away children's toys and evidence of pets, mow the lawn and do the weeding.

- Critically look at the external paintwork, including the fascia boards. When did you last redecorate? Peeling paint is unattractive and gives a strong message that the property is generally neglected.

- Take a good look at the gardens at the back and the sides of the house too. Make sure all the lawns and flower beds are neat and any paved or decked areas have been jet-washed and that moss or algae has been removed. Fences and boundaries should be clearly defined and in good repair.

In Chapter Six, we look at the functionality of your outside spaces and buildings in more detail.

In summary

- Work out who your target buyer is likely to be and look at your home through their eyes.

- Present your rooms in a way that's aimed at your target buyer; let go of your emotional attachment to how your home looks now.

- Photograph your rooms and notice what you see in these photos.

- Be honest with yourself and take advice from a friend, your agent or a professional home stager before the next step.

FOUR

Declutter

M ost of us live with a degree of clutter. I'm sure I'm not alone in the daily challenge of tidying the kitchen only to find the island piled high with 'stuff' the moment my partner or children walk through the door. We keep treasures, mementoes of special moments. We keep souvenirs of happy family holidays and we put paperwork, letters, bills to be paid and old birthday cards into piles while we decide on our filing system. None of this matters until we decide it's time to sell our home and suddenly we need to see our clutter as other people will.

Why can't people see past my stuff?

I explain to vendors daily that while many people find it hard to visualise a house without clutter and with their own furniture installed, even more people simply don't understand why they should have to see past someone else's clutter if that person is serious about selling their house. This is a generation of people who have grown up with television and digital advertising. They're used to businesses competing for their money, and they spend only on products they believe are the best for the task in hand. A property which is cluttered, dated or dirty sends a strong message that the vendor doesn't care about the buyer. They will quickly suspect that the house is probably not well maintained and that the vendor won't be interested enough in them as a buyer to progress the sale quickly and efficiently. You can see how this will rapidly translate into a potential buyer saying no.

WHAT A MESS

Before Lemon and Lime Interiors became a stand-alone business, I was invited to the country home of a woman who was working in London. She had decided to sell and move full time to the city. She was living alone in a four-bedroom home with several cats. In every room there was a pile of papers, folders and textbooks. Every bookcase had files spilling from the shelves, and throughout the house were large plastic boxes – an attempt to control the paperwork – with lids off and paper falling out. Opening any cupboard was impossible; contents welcomed the chance to escape and join the chaos on the floor. On top of this, the smell of cat wee pervaded the space. It was evident that selling the house in this state wouldn't be feasible.

Clearly the vendor was an intelligent woman. And yet, this was her view: 'Anyone coming into the house to view isn't looking at my stuff – they'll only be looking at the location [which was lovely] and the space on offer. I can't tidy up – I won't know where anything is.' None of my arguments changed her mind. My saying that viewers are put off by the smell of pets, regardless of whether they're pet lovers themselves, didn't register. I explained that the clutter made it apparent that there wasn't enough storage in the house for one person living there, so it certainly wouldn't appeal to a family, in spite of the four bedrooms. Nothing helped. That house was one of my failures. I couldn't persuade her to do any work, either with our help or by herself. It took four years to sell and I still have no idea if the vendor had to concede and tidy up before she eventually found her buyer or if she accepted a ridiculously low offer.

SMOOTH MOVE

Conversely, we took on a similar-sized property to help with the decluttering as it came onto the market. It was an Edwardian house close to a town centre – not out of the ordinary until you walked inside. Inside, antique furniture and ornaments were stacked everywhere, and there was barely space to move around the faux-flower arrangements. The vendor's family had found the perfect downsize property for her. It was close to them, to her friends and to shops and health care. They were determined to make the move as smooth as possible while recognising that it would be a huge wrench for her to leave the home she'd loved for more than forty years. Our team spent a week with her, boxing up everything she wanted to take with her and finding new homes, via an auction house, charity shops and family and friends, for much of the surplus furniture and treasures. The house was thoroughly cleaned. It came onto the market with great professional photos and sold within twenty-four hours, allowing the whole family to breathe a huge sigh of relief. By this time, with so much help, the major work for the move had already been done and there was no drawn-out period of viewings and keeping everything tidy. The lack of clutter in this case enabled a new family to see the space on offer and imagine themselves enjoying the lifestyle the beautiful home with its original Edwardian features could offer them.

Clutter

Clutter is emotionally draining. Many psychological studies have identified how too much stuff can trigger feelings of stress and loss of control.[17] Clutter can make us anxious. It is a constant reminder of tasks we have not completed. It is also a huge waste of time. Finding a particular paper under a huge pile is never easy and it is a distraction.

Marie Kondo has built an amazing business around tidying up. She recognises and teaches the art of needing less and feeling freer through the act of getting rid

---

17   www.paw.princeton.edu/article/psychology-your-attention-please

of anything that doesn't create joy in our lives.[18] Home isn't just a place to live and to store our belongings. Home is an environment where we relax, work and enjoy downtime with our loved ones. It's different things to different people, but I've never heard anyone say, 'It's the place where we can dump all our unwanted, unnecessary and unloved stuff and still feel joyful'.

Clutter can make it harder to both enjoy being at home and get tasks done. If there's a pile of washing in the kitchen, it's harder to pour a glass of wine and relax as we cook with the family – the washing basket will always be in our peripheral vision, demanding to be emptied. If we step into our home study to write something, our creativity will be hindered, or jeopardised completely, if we have to first spend an hour tidying the desk.

Our clutter is exhausting, but at least we understand the source of it, even if it's out of control. Think of the last time you walked into a room full of someone else's clutter, though. You might have seen a pile of papers in the corner and wondered about their significance. You might have seen dirty dishes piled in the sink and itched to transfer them into the dishwasher. If there's clutter in a house you're viewing, it's easy to be distracted from your decision to buy if there's tidying that needs to be done. Plus, the house is likely to be dirty as

---

18   Kondo M, *The Life-changing Magic of Tidying: A simple, effective way to banish clutter forever* (Vermilion, 2014)

a result – few people actually clean properly and return clutter to its piles. Clutter and dirt will quickly change an interested prospective purchaser into one who says a firm 'No thank you'.

The psychological impact of clutter goes a long way to explain why homes full of knick-knacks, books and papers without a place are so difficult to sell. Fortunately, if you think ahead and aren't intending to approach an agent or launch your property to the market within a few hours of making the decision to move, clutter can be fixed. It's usually a matter of time, energy and motivation. Below, we'll look at the practical steps you can take to remove the clutter and get your home into show home style.

Sorting your belongings

Walk through your house slowly, notebook in hand. Write down the strengths and the challenges you see in each room regarding clutter. Don't forget the hallway, stairs and landing. Consider the areas of your home as someone else might see them. Notice where bookcases are overfull or wardrobes are bursting at the seams. Remember, at some point in the near future you'll be packing everything. If an item is not going to be useful in the next few weeks or enhance the appearance of a room in a positive way, it needs to go. You might want to bear in mind the William Morris quote as you go through this process: 'Have nothing in your house that you do not know to be useful or believe to be beautiful.'[19]

You have three options for your belongings:

- Skip
- Store
- Show

Skip is the option for any items you don't need or want to keep when you move. You may wish to give someone else a chance to own these items through an auction house or by selling online. You can also take them to a local charity shop – some will even collect from you. You may choose to give things away on a free local recycling site. Sort through the piles of things that you no longer want as your first step. Once you've started to move some of the clutter from the house, you'll quickly find that your headspace is clearer and you can decide what you really need to keep while you're on the market. For many people, decluttering has been on a to-do list for years – this is great motivation.

The next step is to store anything you're not using regularly, perhaps in a garage or garden shed. Remember, though, that these spaces are also spaces that your viewers will want to see. Increasingly, since COVID-19,

---

19   Todd, P, *William Morris and the Arts and Crafts Home* (Thames and Hudson, 2012)

people are thinking of what could be used as a home office or a hobby room. Off-site storage, either with a friend or family member or at a storage facility, may be your best option. Do think ahead, in case your sale takes a few months – what might you need soon that you don't need now? Also make sure that anything going into storage is labelled carefully. You don't want to have to sort through every single box to find the outfit you bought for a friend's wedding.

THE IMPORTANCE OF LABELLING

One family we helped put a lot of their belongings into storage in the early part of the summer. Three months later, as the solicitors were finalising the sale's contractual elements, the family called me to ask if I'd seen the children's school shoes. Term had begun again after the summer holidays, but the winter shoes had all been sent into storage. It was quicker to buy new ones than to search through all the unlabelled boxes.

At this stage, you'll need a lot of boxes and bubble wrap. In my case, I also need a lot of coffee, some great music and some friends to help. Wrapping china, the huge serving bowls that only come out at Christmas, the crystal glasses that were a wedding present and the souvenir ornaments the children bought during a lovely holiday is much more fun if it isn't tackled alone. Finally, keep to hand all the things you use daily. It's important to keep the house looking loved. We have worked with people who have taken decluttering to an extreme. Depersonalising a home to the point where it feels cold and slightly sterile will never capture the heart of your buyer. We always advise keeping a few family photos around, ensuring that bookcases are about two-thirds full and positioning ornaments or flower arrangements strategically on display shelves. The interior designer's rule of three applies here – objects look best grouped in odd numbers; usually one isn't enough and seven are too many but three or even five work well.

If you're still living in the home and are engaging a home stager's services, it's important that you get on with them. Decluttering is a personal experience. We certainly try to match our team to our clients. Some clients respond best to my directness: 'Oh my goodness, you can't possibly sell a house that looks like this.' Others need Kate's more measured approach: 'Well, I think perhaps we might be able to help you get ready for your move by starting to pack a few things in boxes.'

Smells don't sell

When getting a house ready for sale, vendors often forget one of the most important senses: smell. Let's face it, after years of living in your house, you've probably become used to the smell, whether it's good or bad. Ask a close friend to be honest and tell you if they can smell dog, damp, smoke or anything else that's less than pleasant when they come to your home.

A bad smell is one of the single biggest turn-offs for prospective buyers. Don't try to mask the smell with heavy sprays or even candles and diffusers. Identify the source then fix it by cleaning bins and drains, opening windows and washing pet bedding. Pet litter trays and food bowls should live outside during viewings. Someone who doesn't live with animals will always be put off by the smells associated with them.

I was invited to a home which should have been an easy sell for the agent. It was in a popular area, near good schools and offered practical accommodation for a family. The agent knew what the problem was but couldn't bear to tell the owners – they thought they would lose the instruction – so they asked me to take a look. The moment I opened the front door I knew what was putting off prospective buyers. The smell of cigarette smoke was overwhelming to the point I could hardly bear to go inside. Astonishingly, the owners were oblivious to the smell. I can't say they were exactly grateful for my advice when I told them, but at least they could make a decision about what to do.

Top tips for eliminating bad smells

Once you have identified the cause of a bad smell in your home then you can use the appropriate method to get to rid of it. Some smells are simple, remove the cause and the smell goes, others linger and you need to tackle what is left behind.

- If you're a smoker, place bowls of vinegar around the house and leave out for three days. Although the vinegar has a strong scent, when you open the windows it will disappear quickly, taking away most of the stale cigarette smell with it. Remove furniture in which the smoke smell is embedded and get your carpets professionally cleaned.

- Pet odour can usually be eliminated by taking food bowls and litter trays outside. The lingering pet smells can usually be addressed by using a local carpet and upholstery cleaning service.

- If your house smells of damp and you haven't been able to have the damp treated, leaving a bowl of clean cat litter on top of a cupboard close to the source will help. Cat litter absorbs damp air after a few days.

- Sadly, houses being sold as part of an estate of someone who is deceased often smell. Changing the carpets is usually the best solution. The cost of doing so should be regarded as an investment – it will significantly increase the house's saleability.

- To tackle fridge odours, open a box of baking soda and pop it on a shelf or along the back. Change it monthly and keep it away from vegetables, since sodium bicarbonate can cause leafy veggies to wilt quickly. Sodium bicarbonate has a unique chemical property that attracts and absorbs odours.

- Cooking smells (especially if you make a lot of spicy or fried foods) can become ingrained in your cabinets. Wash them with warm water and soap and leave doors and windows open for as long as possible ahead of any viewings to get rid of these smells.

Top tips for creating good smells

A good smell can make your property feel welcoming. Here are some age-old tips:

- Bake bread or cake.

- Brew coffee before a viewing.

- Use gorgeous smelling diffusers around the house. If you use the same fragrance in all the main rooms, viewers will remember your home above any others. Cheap diffusers smell horrible, as do many of the chemical plug-in versions. Next and John Lewis are our favourite high street suppliers of reed diffusers. If you can't get hold of this type and quality, then don't use anything – just let fresh air into every room before your viewings.

- Bathrooms need to smell fresh. Good old-fashioned bleach in the loo works wonders. If you have a rarely used bathroom, be aware of the smell that stagnant water left sitting in the U-bend of the waste pipe creates. Running water through to ensure any standing water is clean will do the trick if this is the case.

In summary

- Declutter everywhere and then declutter again. Your viewers shouldn't have to see past your stuff to visualise how the house could be if only it were tidy.

- Bookcases and wardrobes should be about two-thirds full, no more.

- Tackle any smells in the house. A bad smell is one of the most off-putting factors for a potential buyer.

- Carpets and pets are the biggest culprits when it comes to unpleasant smells.

FIVE

Decorate

This chapter talks you through the best way to redecorate before your sale, should you need to. You may not need this chapter at all. Many of the homes we go to for a first consultation have been beautifully decorated within the last five years or so. The walls are based on a neutral palette and all the accent colours flow throughout the house. These touches mean that the home already feels calm and well maintained, even if there's still decluttering to be done or a few pieces of furniture that need to be replaced. If this is the case for you, please feel free to skip to the next chapter.

About half the homes we see don't fall into this category. It may be that they haven't been painted for a while or that there are some repairs that have been neglected for several years. Occasionally, we see real horrors.

COLOUR DISASTER

I visited a four-bedroom home in a great location. Once three separate cottages, it had been turned into a single property with huge rooms and some lovely features. But the owners had painted the entire open-plan space on the ground floor orange. I don't mean a gentle orangey off-white – I mean orange. Including the ceilings. As I sat down to chat with them about how we could help with their sale, Annie, the vendor said, 'The only thing I'm not prepared to do is redecorate. I love orange.' I finished my coffee and politely explained that there was no point in spending any money doing anything else. Six months later, Annie phoned. The house was still on the market and had received little interest from potential buyers. 'Okay, what colour do you suggest?' We compromised – the ceiling was painted white and the walls a soft white with a slightly orange tone. The owners achieved their sale within four weeks and set off on their dream trip around the world.

Refreshing tired decor

When I visit someone's home for the first time to do a consultation, I can often tell when they moved in and certainly the last time they decorated. There are two aspects to this: colours and the general state of the decor. You'll need to address both. Be honest – have you talked yourself out of redecorating, saying, 'There's no point because a new owner will only come in and re-do it to their taste'? Out of the houses we see where the decorating is an issue, at least 80% of vendors tell us this. The message you're giving to your potential buyer is this: 'The decor is dated and tired, so you'll need to paint as soon as you move in. The cost of redecorating will add several hundred (or thousand) pounds over and above what you pay for the house.' You're not ensuring your buyer feels as though they are part of the win-win-win situation we discussed in Chapter One. It may also be that they choose to offer significantly less than your guide price, reflecting the money they believe they'll need to spend on redecorating.

A quick note on wallpaper. If your walls are papered and you need to redecorate you have a choice. If the wallpaper is a fairly light colour and in good repair, you can paint over it. It may take an extra coat, but this will be much quicker and more cost effective than stripping it off. If it's damaged or the colour and texture don't allow for painting over the top, be prepared to skim the walls underneath, or perhaps go over the top with lining paper. Old houses in particular will need a degree of replastering if wallpaper is taken off. It's likely that at least some of the old plaster will come away with the wallpaper.

Colour

Colours go in and out of fashion in interiors almost as quickly as they do in clothes. Since I started styling homes for sale in earnest, we have gone through various trends: aubergine, mustard, navy, bottle greens and soft pinks. Of course, this keeps my designers interested and loving their job. I still get excited when one of them brings me a mood board for a show home with colours we haven't yet used but which are trending in the interiors magazines that pile up in our office. There are many aspects to colour, and it's a subject I could easily get distracted enough by to write another book. Let's stick to three themes that you need to consider if you're looking to achieve a great sale:

- Fashion
- Light
- Period

Fashion

In general, the solution to the colour dilemma has been 'paint everything neutral'. Hmmm, okay. But bizarrely, neutrals are just as susceptible to the vagaries of fashion as other colours. Pick up any paint chart or look up 'neutral paint colour' in a search engine and you'll be overwhelmed with choices.

I was horrified to hear that an agent with whom we occasionally work told one of their vendors, 'You don't need to call Lemon and Lime – just paint all the walls magnolia.' Ah! Magnolia as a base colour went about fifteen years ago. It's one of the fastest ways of dating a property and can make a place look as though it has been lived in by heavy smokers for a long time.

Grey has been a popular neutral in the last decade. But which grey? It can be difficult to choose the right shade, and it's probably influenced more than any other neutral by light and the period in which your home was built.

An interior designer might be appalled by the technique of picking the 'colour of the year' for your walls. Whatever this colour happens to be, it ends up being overused and eventually dismissed by professionals. That said, you want to make your home appeal to as many buyers as possible in the shortest possible time. Choosing a popular colour may also send a subliminal message to your buyers that the house is cared for and switched on to contemporary trends. This isn't the time to be alternative or bohemian in your choices.

RIGHT HOUSE, WRONG GREY

Years ago, we were involved with a three-bedroom home in a nice village close to our office. The family had relocated for work and taken all the furniture with them. Before they left, they redecorated the whole house in a fashionable grey. The house was still on the market four months later and there was little interest in it, so we were called in to see if we could shed some light on what the problem might be.

The colour in itself was perfect and in many houses would have been the right solution. In this house, though, the main source of natural light was from the north, the direction the front room faced. The grey just looked depressing because the light was so poor.

And as there was no furniture, there was nothing to showcase the lifestyle the property offered. Our first step was to paint the walls a soft off-white in a cream palette, not grey. We then furnished the house. A week or so later, the estate agent told me she'd practically had to move into the house, given how many viewings she was doing. An offer was accepted within two weeks of the changes being made.

The message is clear: choose not only a fashionable neutral to spruce up your decor ahead of a sale but also ensure it suits the light in your home. Finding out what's in style is fairly simple. Buy a few home decoration magazines, anything from *Elle Decoration* to *Ideal Home*, settle down with a cup of coffee or a glass of wine and leaf through, taking note of the main wall colours. Most magazines will detail which paint has been used. Steer clear of the bright colours and glitzy wallpaper but consider any neutrals that appear more than once.

Light

The second element in your colour decision is light, which is affected by your house's location and orientation.

Location

Is your home on the coast, in the countryside or in the city? Your surroundings will affect the quality of light you're able to bring inside. I was brought up on the coast in Norfolk, where the light is strong and clear. Norfolk has a lot of sky. I now live in rural Derbyshire. I said to a client one day, 'Well of course the problem that I'm having is that there's no light here.' She didn't understand what I meant. Not uniquely, many Derbyshire houses are built in a dip. Historically this served to protect them from the worst of the wind and weather, but it also means that the light entering the houses is limited. Country houses, in a dip or not, generally benefit from a lot of green outside. Top tip: don't paint using 'beachy' colours if you're surrounded by green – it looks weird. Interestingly, city homes, surrounded by a much greyer landscape, can look amazing in cold grey neutrals or even white. Here, the use of accent colours is key. And in my view, a city apartment is the only property you can market with a full monochrome scheme and attract significant interest. It fits with the landscape.

Orientation

You need to consider how light moves around your home throughout the day. The season you plan to be marketing your home will also affect the quality of light. Try to decorate close to the start date of marketing if you need to change your wall colours. Winter colours should be warmer, summer colours cooler, as a rule of thumb. If you're not sure where the light comes from at different times of day, use a compass app on your phone to figure it out. If the light moves around the house so that the main rooms have light from the south for a large proportion of the day, you'll need to use different colours than those used for a home which has its dominant light from the north or the east.

The best way to tell for sure is to get some sample pots and paint two-foot squares in different colours on each wall of the room you'll be redecorating. You can't fight the light in your home, so work with it. Check which colour you prefer at different times of day for a few days and ask family members or friends who visit to comment; make sure you write down preferences. Within a few days, you'll be sure of the choice with the most appeal. This is the one you should use. Remember, you're aiming for mass market appeal, not choosing a colour you plan to live with forever.

DON'T FIGHT IT

One client was determined that by engaging my help I'd be able to make her sitting room a light, bright space. She was frustrated when I explained that there was nothing I could do to change the fact that the room had east-facing windows and natural light coming in from the north. Nothing I did would make the room bright in the evening, which was when the room was used the most. My advice was to paint the walls a warm neutral. The Farrow & Ball colour Elephant's Breath has been a warm neutral favourite for a long time. Accenting the decor with deep-teal soft furnishings really brought the room to life and made it feel like a cosy family room.

The years she'd spent fighting against the natural light were counterproductive.

Period

The third consideration when choosing a colour is the period of your home. In the late eighties and early nineties, it was fashionable to paint period homes in heritage colours. Many homes, including mine, had deep red dining rooms and sunny yellow kitchens. Some still have them. This isn't a good look for your sale. In the current market, these colours in general are no longer desirable.

A GOOD COMPROMISE

One lovely eighteenth-century cottage we worked on had deep red walls, rich orange walls (and ceilings) and a lot of dark green paint on the walls of the halls and landings. It had been on the market for about eighteen months when we were asked to comment on what changes we would advise. While it seemed obvious from my point of view, the owner was reluctant to redecorate the whole house. Eventually we picked out a Dulux colour called Almond White and made a compromise. He painted the main rooms in this colour and the ceilings this colour everywhere else. The house was sold before the new brochure came back from the printers.

When it comes to wall colour:

- Cooler colours look great in modern coastal homes and city apartments.

- Countryside and period homes generally look better with warmer tones.

- Ordinary, pure, brilliant white in a matte finish is the easiest colour to work with in new builds but can reveal a whole range of bumps in walls in an older home.

Accent colours

Accent colours are the colours we use for soft furnishings and accessories. They might be found in a piece of artwork or a quirky armchair. These are the colours that bring life to a home. It's easy to change the feel of a room completely by changing the accent colour.

Here's a general guideline to follow when thinking about how to involve colour in a space:

- 60% – the main colour

- 30% – a secondary colour

- 10% – an accent colour

The secondary colours we suggest are usually a shade of the main colour, perhaps slightly darker. Or they may be a slightly different tone. We might pair a dark grey floor with soft white walls. In a house for sale it works for the secondary colour to also be a neutral. The secondary and the main colour may also appear in the soft furnishings alongside the accent colour.

When we're working with a client to prepare a home for sale, we make sure there's an accent colour for the house. If the house is occupied, this colour will be chosen based on something the client already has, perhaps a favourite painting or a sofa. If the house is empty, we have freer rein.

We follow trends carefully, as you can imagine, and we like to experiment. It's easy to swap out a few cushions if we get it wrong. My advice to my designers is always to choose one accent colour for the whole house. If the colour is blue, we'll work with tones of blue in each room. Working with tones of one colour throughout the house gives the space a sense of calm. Remember, we're talking about accent colours here – I'm not suggesting you repaint your whole house one colour! Many people notice colour on a subconscious level. If you go into a house which has yellows in one room, pinks in another and reds in yet another, you'll come out buzzing (not in a good way).

This isn't to say that when you're living in your home you shouldn't experiment with lots of colours. If you like bright colours and rooms in different colours, go for it. The point here is that you want to attract as many potential buyers as possible – and most people want their homes to be a sanctuary at the end of a busy day. If they leave your viewing feeling this way about your home, they'll come back and perhaps be tempted to put in that all-important offer.

The investment you make in new cushions and a few accessories will pay dividends. Flat cushions are never a good look but are inevitable in a home with children and dogs. New ones, even ones you keep in a box especially for photos and viewings, will make a big difference. Your accent colour may be dictated by colours you already have in expensive items such as curtains. Bear this in mind, but also remember that while your house is on the market, you could do a simple fix. An alternative to replacing expensive curtains, especially for a summer sale, may be to switch them for plain voile panels hung from a pole. These always look fresh and bright. If you have neutral walls and simple curtains, you can choose your colour with confidence. (Oh, but don't choose red! Red never photographs well. It's a distraction and for some reason always looks dated.)

Tricks with colour

Colour can deceive the eye, and it's worth knowing which tricks can be played honestly.

- The lighter the colour, the bigger a room will appear.

- Darker colours can help make a room with poor natural light feel cosier.

- A white ceiling will seem higher and bring more space into a room.

- If your ceiling is high and you want to 'bring it down' to make a room feel more welcoming, paint the ceiling or the area above the picture rail a warmer white.

- Feature walls go in and out of fashion quickly – avoid them if you're redecorating.

Woodwork

The woodwork on the skirting boards, architrave and window frames is something else you may need to think about while you are considering any redecorating. I can't tell you how many bannisters and skirting boards we've taken from dark brown varnish to white eggshell paint – and in doing so, without making any other changes, we see offers materialise.

GOOD TIMING

One of the first homes I prepared for sale was for a friend who had moved abroad. The house had the orange pine skirting boards and doors so popular in the late eighties and early nineties. The change in taking all that wood to white paint was dramatic. Suddenly, everything looked fresher and, bizarrely, more spacious. The house was one of my early success stories and launched me on the path of setting up Lemon and Lime Interiors. It eventually sold for about £50K more than the agents had been prepared to list it for. This had all happened because one day, I'd happened to drive past and see the For Sale board. I called my friend and told her she couldn't possibly sell the house in the state it appeared to be in if the garden was anything to go by. She gave me free rein to sort it out. It took about £12K of work, including redecoration all the way through. This proved to be well worth the spend and the effort, attracting competing buyers at a time when the market was flat (the winter of 2011/12).

If your woodwork is already white, or your doors are made of a fashionable wood (do your research), check for scuff marks and scratches. If you haven't noticed these in your day-to-day wanderings, take a closer look. Paintwork will inevitably get bashed, perhaps by the Hoover or by keys or handbags or rings. My younger son keeps his bike in the hallway when he's home, and this marks up the walls. Apparently, the bike is far too precious to live in the garage. I keep a small roller and tin of paint to hand and whizz over the wall every time he goes away again, taking his bike with him.

Tired-looking decor will form a huge part of the first impression a viewer has of your home. If a prospective buyer notices a lot of scuff marks throughout the house, they'll question how well the parts of the house they can't see at first glance are maintained. They may wonder if the roof is in need of repair, or when you last had the electrical wiring checked. These questions will loom large in their mind once they've left the viewing. If the next house they view has been decorated recently, it may suddenly jump ahead of yours on their list. At this stage, make sure all the decorating and minor repairs have been done so you're not giving your viewers any cause for concern.

Repairs

At this stage in the process, you also need to make sure repairs (major or minor) are done. Kitchen cupboard doors hanging off, squeaky gates, a patch of damp on the chimney breast – these are all things that your buyer will notice. And many buyers, especially if they've never done any DIY in the past, will be put off. They'll imagine that the cost of repair is greater than it actually is and won't want the hassle. Even if you think your buyer is likely to rip out the kitchen and replace it, get the existing one repaired. No one wants to live, even on a temporary basis, with stained worktops or damaged tiles.

The grout in showers needs to be spotless. It might be a matter of scrubbing with one of the specialist products on the market, or you could simply use bleach. If the problem is quite bad, you may need to regrout between the tiles. Again, this shouldn't be an expensive job but does make a world of difference. In the Assess stage, you will have noted all the repairs that need to be done. Now is the time to do them.

Kitchens

We see a lot of kitchens that need updating. Naturally, most vendors don't want the big expense of replacing a kitchen just before they sell. Our top tip is to paint the cabinets. Painted kitchens are more often in fashion than not and work particularly well in country homes. If your kitchen is of the nineties wood era, either dark oak or pine, you can paint the doors in any colour you like. Again, a neutral is favourable but you may choose to use an accent colour for a few cupboards or on an island. Changing the handles and knobs is another quick fix that will transform the look of a kitchen for minimal expense. You can buy lovely ones either online or at stores such as TK Maxx or B&Q.

Another quick fix is the worktop. An old-fashioned Formica worktop (I'm not talking about the retro version that's recently become popular again) can easily be changed. So can cheap-looking, dark granite from the 1980s. An oak block or even a composite worktop can be cut around your existing sink and hob and will transform the kitchen's working area. Another top tip: go for a chunkier depth than standard. It instantly updates a kitchen. Hobs, ovens and sinks can be changed too, all for far less cost than replacing the whole kitchen.

Tiles aren't necessary between a worktop and wall cupboards. An upstand in the same material as the worktop is fashionable. If you've damaged tiles while taking off your worktop, don't worry. Repair the wall and put a 100-millimetre upstand behind the worktop instead.

Bathrooms

Dated avocado, pink and peach bathrooms still appear more often than I'd like in properties for sale. Retro shades may be *en vogue* in super-fashionable circles, but white still wins the mainstream vote. Vendors will ask me, 'Should I change the bathroom?' I'm more likely to say yes to this than to changing a kitchen, but it depends on the state of the rest of the house and on the house's value.

If yours is a project house (see Chapter Three), don't change the bathroom. Your buyer is someone who will be completely renovating. If the rest of the house is lovely but you never quite got round to changing the bathroom, now is your moment. You will recoup the cost in a better sale.

Bathroom suites should be white. Wall tiles are most desirable in large format and light in colour. Floors need to be tiled or good quality vinyl, depending on house value. If yours is a family house, there should be at least one bath. A family with small children may well prefer a bath over a shower. If you're selling an apartment to first-time buyers and have one small bathroom, a shower rather than a bath is fine. Always keep in mind who your most likely buyer will be.

My final point about bathrooms is the floor. We still see bathrooms with carpet on the floors, and in some cases, carpet up the side of the bath. Carpet on a bathroom floor is one of the most impractical features in a home. It gets soggy and soggy carpet smells. Good quality vinyl or tiles are relatively inexpensive. If your bathroom has a carpeted floor, you will get a good return on the small investment you make in changing for hard flooring ahead of your sale.

In summary

- Redecorate if you have dated decor or a lot of strong colours on your walls.

- Ceilings should be white or another light colour.

- Not every neutral suits every house – do your homework.

- Choose the same neutral for all the rooms you're repainting ahead of your sale.

- Choose an accent colour for the whole house and use tones of it to create a sense of calm.

- Repainting wooden kitchen cabinets can give them a whole new lease of life.

- Update a kitchen quickly by changing the worktop and appliances.

- Update your bathroom if the rest of the house looks great but your bathroom suite is coloured.

- The bathroom and kitchen should have hard flooring, not carpet.

SIX

Re-Imagine And Emphasise

O ur homes are the places we relax, where we nurture our family and entertain our friends. They may also be our place of work in a post-COVID-19 world. When someone is looking for a new home these will all be functions they have in mind. Your challenge as a vendor is to show how your home is the place that offers the perfect blend of space.

Re-imagine – Creating functionality and flow

Houses evolve as families evolve. It's entirely normal for a small sitting room to go from being a family TV room to being a playroom, a study and then, perhaps, a downstairs bedroom for an elderly parent. We see houses where beautiful Victorian dining rooms with all their original features are being used as game rooms for teenage children.

LOCAL PUB?

We once saw a Victorian dining room that had taken on the feel of an old-school pub, complete with wallpaper the colour of nicotine-stained walls. The atmosphere of the room created the feeling that a viewer would need to battle a fog of cigarette smoke to enter. We painted the ceiling white and the walls a gentler off-white than the previous dark cream, and this completely changed the room. We also added a dining table in place of the snooker table, and suddenly we'd created a desirable family home.

I've seen a utility room with all the appliances removed being used as a dog kennel for large, smelly dogs. I've seen rooms in lived-in homes that have become nothing more than dumping grounds.

Viewers often find it hard to visualise a room with a function it doesn't have in that moment. You will significantly increase your chances of attracting your buyer if every room in your home has a clear, logical function. Ask your agent, a friend or a professional stager for advice if you don't know what function a particular room should have for the market you're aiming for. A second or third reception room may need to be transformed into a home office or a gym.

Or perhaps a sixth bedroom could become a dressing room or even a cinema room.

A MATTER OF PERSPECTIVE

The example that drove the point about functionality home to me was a property we were asked to help with that had been on the market for about six months. The vendors had moved out and left some but not all the furniture. The house was in a good village and had great views from the big open-plan kitchen/living room. It should have sold in no time.

I asked, as I always do, what the feedback had been from the viewings so far. Not just one but several of the viewers had told the agent that the dining room was too far from the kitchen. When I saw the house, I had to chuckle. It was such a perfect example of how viewers simply can't see beyond what's there. The kitchen was huge – it had a dining area and plenty of room for sofas too. Next to the kitchen was a completely empty room and further along the hallway was a big room divided by bifold doors. The owners had left their dining furniture in this room. It was where they preferred to eat if they were entertaining. Funnier still, when I suggested to the owners that, as part of our work, we would move dining furniture into the empty room next to the kitchen, they told me quite firmly that that room wasn't the dining room, it was the study.

If people have lived in a particular way for a long time, it's hard to see their own home differently, and it feels challenging when a complete stranger walks in and moves things around. Happily, we did end up moving the table and chairs, and also put furniture into the other empty rooms in the house, and a buyer came along quickly. The dining room was no longer too far from the kitchen – it was now in the room next to the kitchen that had previously been empty.

Bedrooms are an interesting case. Often, especially once the children have left a home, a bedroom may acquire another function. I've seen several homes where a bedroom has been converted into a dressing room to serve the main bedroom. In some cases, this is a good use of space and will add to the house's saleability. This is especially true if the house has four other bedrooms. Generally, going from five to six bedrooms doesn't change the value of a house significantly. But taking a house from four bedrooms to three bedrooms by creating a dressing room or an office will almost always impact the saleability. A four-bedroom property will command a higher price than one with three bedrooms. Think carefully about how you use the rooms, and ask your agent, or a professional stager, for their thoughts. A stager can help you convert any room back to a bedroom with minimum fuss. Oh, and remember, a bedroom isn't a bedroom unless it has a bed in it!

Your main aim is to create a logical flow of living accommodation. The dining room should be close to the kitchen. A study or home office shouldn't take up a second reception room at the expense of a second sitting room or a snug. A study can occupy a third reception room, fifth bedroom or part of an open-plan space. A playroom can be combined with a study or a snug but shouldn't be a dedicated room except in the largest houses. And a games room or a gym is best suited to the second floor of a house (if there are at least four bedrooms on the first floor) or in the garage or an outbuilding. If any of these additional 'luxury' spaces are important to a viewer, they will understand that once they move in, the space can be repurposed into a room for their own needs.

Functionality outside

Pre-COVID-19, many agents and vendors didn't pay much attention to a property's exterior beyond ensuring it was tidy and looked well kept. As home stagers, we might have suggested that a garage or a summer house be used temporarily for storing clutter. The global pandemic changed this view. Now there are far more viewers looking for homes that have multi-functionality. More people will be viewing their homes as their office, gym and social space.

GETTING CREATIVE

We helped a couple, Helen and Mike, move quickly from their home on a new estate in Derby. It looked much the same as all the other homes on the street, and there were several for sale on the estate at the time. Helen and Mike wanted to sell quickly and move into the annex of the home their son was building. We did some work inside to ensure everything was presented to its best, but they didn't need much help here.

Mike's garage was a different story. It was full of old pots of paint, bags of useful string and parts of a motorbike that had long since been sold. (I'm hopeful the motorbike received new parts to replace those still in the garage.) I felt that we could use the garage to make this property stand out against the others on the street.

We tidied, threw out everything that no longer seemed to have a purpose and positioned Mike's pride and joy, an old E-Type Jag, for photos. Then we had another idea. We cleaned the tool bench which stretched across the length of the garage at the back, carefully positioned tools on it and brought in a big leather armchair and the coffee machine from the house. Suddenly, this normal garage was transformed into a great workspace with all the comforts anyone could need. It wasn't complicated or expensive, but the house attracted an offer within days.

WORK WITH WHAT YOU HAVE

A similar thing happened when we helped a family clear their barn of years of clutter. It had been used as a dumping ground for every bike the kids had grown out of, every half-roll of unused wallpaper and every electrical appliance that needed fixing. Two skips later and the space we opened up was amazing. We uncovered racks on the wall and hung the family kayaks.

We put two state-of-the-art road bikes back on their stands and had a professional photographer photograph the barn. It attracted so much interest that the family moved into their new home a good six months earlier than anticipated. We showed an aspect that is often forgotten but now, more than ever, has enormous value in terms of saleability. Many people aspire to an outdoor lifestyle and the ability to spend time as a family pursuing activities. This often requires lots of equipment. Buying a home with plenty of dedicated storage can suddenly transport the imagination of a viewer into their new life in your home.

Suddenly, a summer house has potential as a home gym. A reception room becomes both a playroom and a home school with a big screen for movies and lessons. I recently saw a cellar which had had the walls lined and waterproofed and made into a cosy cinema room.

Could you dig a small vegetable patch in an unused corner of the garden or put in a couple of raised beds? Lettuce grows quickly at the right time of year. Remember, you want to create as much emotional connection for your prospective buyer with your home as you possibly can. One home we saw had a small wood at the bottom of a paddock belonging to the house. We photographed a tent and firepit in the wood to inspire a family looking to buy in that area to think about the adventures they could have without leaving their own land. If you're lucky enough to be selling a house with land and perhaps space for horses, tidy up.

Stables should be immaculate; everything in the tack room needs to have a place. These homes are usually high value – there's no excuse for leaving their working areas in a mess. Your stables and tack room set the scene for an aspirational lifestyle. Someone moving to the country for the first time might be able to afford your home but will be put off by too much reality of the country life.

Emphasise – selling the lifestyle

Once you've clearly established the purpose of each room, it's time to take stock and decide which features of your home you want to emphasise and which ones you'd like to draw attention away from, if possible. You're telling your buyer a story of how their life will look once they've bought your home. A buyer's first impression of every room is from the doorway, so their heart must be captured as they stand in the entrance. Walk around your home taking the route you'd like your viewers to take. Pause in each doorway and notice what you see. Could you arrange the furniture more favourably? Would a well-placed flower arrangement or dramatic vase change the room's emphasis to make it more interesting? Or do you need to move a few things out of the immediate line of sight? Our brains can process only a small proportion of the information they see at any one time. We refer to the excess as 'visual noise' and try to calm it down.

What lovely moments have you enjoyed while living in your home? How might you tell the story to a viewer or to someone looking at your photos online?

Perhaps there's a corner of the garden that catches the evening sun where you enjoy a glass of wine in the summer, or perhaps you have a gorgeous fireplace in the sitting room which could be lit when your potential buyers come around. A professional stager will have an informed opinion about what's important and how to emphasise the strongest features of your home. They'll also have a number of tricks up their sleeve, from popping a tray with fresh coffee and croissants on the bed in the main bedroom to stacking beautiful coffee table books in the sitting room next to a bottle of wine and some glasses. People often ask me, 'Can't viewers see past obvious "stages"?' Yes, many viewers do realise that the home has been dressed specifically to show it off, but their emotional engagement happens largely on a subconscious level, so they'll go away remembering the lovely feeling they had in your home.

Three main areas

There are three main areas which are generally accepted as being key to getting your buyer. The kitchen/living room, the main bedroom and the bathrooms. If you don't have the time or energy to do anything else, focus your attention here.

The kitchen/living room

Over the last ten years or so, the trend has been for open-plan living downstairs. A kitchen big enough for a dining table and some family seating has been crucial to the sale of bigger family homes. But trends change, and we're now seeing a slow trend towards people asking for a separate reception room. This is usually in addition to an open-plan kitchen. I hope we'll never return to the days where the kitchen is the dark room at the back of the house where the food is produced by the wife or the servants.

If you're lucky enough to have an open-plan room of this kind, ensure all the areas are distinct. The dining table should look like a dining table, not the space where you're building a cottage industry or where the kids do their homework amid old pizza boxes and soft drink cans. The sofas should look as if a family can sit on them – not as if they're solely the domain of large dogs or an ancient cat. You may believe that your viewers will imagine your furniture gone and theirs in place, but this rarely proves to be true. They will be put off by the story of family life you're tacitly narrating and buy the show home on the neighbouring estate even though the house is smaller and doesn't have the fantastic garden yours offers.

Buyers are smart. They realise that your house probably offers better value for their money, but they simply don't have the time or the energy to make the changes they perceive to be necessary from what you've shown them. It's much easier and more cost effective for you to make the changes before you come onto the market so that people can buy what they're looking for. Remember the win-win-win scenario we created in Chapter One.

If your home doesn't have an open-plan kitchen/living room, then unless the separate rooms are big, you may well have trouble attracting a buyer for a family home. In this case, although it may seem a radical solution, it's worth talking to a builder to see what could be done to open up the space. I advised on one in a great area in Cheshire, an estate-built four-bedroom house, built in the days when kitchens were separate, although this one had already opened the dining/sitting room into one larger room. My strong advice was to take out the stud wall dividing the kitchen from the remainder of the downstairs living space and refit a new kitchen. The difference here wasn't about price (though after the work had been done, the property went back on the market with an increase of almost double the cost of doing the work) – it was about getting a sale at all. The house had been stuck for a long time and went within weeks of the work being done.

Bedrooms

An en-suite bathroom makes a main bedroom much more desirable. Even quite small new-build properties are being built with en-suite bathrooms in at least one bedroom. Creating one bathroom per two bedrooms will significantly increase the appeal of your home. Storage is also important. Older homes are often at a huge advantage over new builds in this regard – they were built in the days when space wasn't at such a premium and building costs weren't so high. They often have plenty of space for wardrobes and several chests of drawers. Many of the homes we see also have dressing rooms. These are a positive selling feature only if they're kept obsessively tidy. The average dressing room we see doesn't come close to this description and should be left with the door firmly closed! Tidying a dressing room requires investment in matching coat hangers, boxes for shoes and hooks for ties, scarves and handbags. Most of us live with wardrobes and dressing rooms that have evolved with none of these things. If you have a great dressing room, make the investment in the small things before you sell – they'll make a big difference.

Imagine the feeling you get when you walk into the bedroom in your favourite hotel. What triggers that feeling? I guarantee it won't be wrinkled bed linen and a chair stacked with someone else's clothes. And yet, this is what many bedrooms look like as viewers walk in. If you're serious about engaging your viewer's emotions to convert them quickly into your buyer, make your bedrooms look like those in a boutique hotel. Buy huge white heavy-cotton bedspreads, as well as some throws and cushions (make sure to pick an accent colour for each of your bedrooms). Give every bed the hotel treatment. We advise against getting new duvet covers in a lived-in home, as it's hard to keep them looking fresh and crisp. No one has time to do an hour of ironing ahead of every viewing. Show homes might go for the 'double duvet' look, but as soon as viewers allow their children to sit on the beds – or worse, jump on them – it's back to the ironing board! Your main bedroom should be a sanctuary of calm: immaculately tidy with a beautifully dressed bed. You're offering your viewer their favourite hotel experience every day if they buy your home.

The bathroom

Before photos and viewings, you need to go to town on your bathrooms. Bathrooms are personal spaces – we spend our time in them mostly naked, tending to the needs of our bodies. Yuck! Get rid of everything personal from the room. I mean everything. We advise our clients to put all their toiletries, soap dishes, sponges and towels in a large lidded plastic box ahead of viewings. Out of this box, before putting the contents of your bathroom into it, will come your 'viewing kit'. At Lemon and Lime Interiors we're big fans of the classic

SELL HIGH, SELL FAST

look. It won't offend anyone and is always *en vogue*. This consists of brand-new white towels and luxury-brand soap and hand cream. We favour The White Company, but Molton Brown or any of the brands you'll find in a good department store can create a spa feeling in your bathroom – even if you've never had time to enjoy it yourself! In our world, towels, bed linen and flowers exist only in white. Fragrance can be added with a diffuser, never air freshener, and if there's an empty shelf or windowsill, you can place a fresh or high-quality faux plant. All your 'viewing kit' (or 'instant transformation kit') items can be returned to their box immediately following viewings so they retain their pristine appearance.

Once you've tackled the main rooms, it's time to make sure you've found all the areas that will sell the story of the fabulous lifestyle your buyer can enjoy once they've bought from you. Think about the place you most love to curl up with a book when you have a quiet minute. Perhaps a chair in a corner of the bedroom or a window seat in the dining room? What about the spot you sit on a sunny Saturday evening with your glass of wine? These are the areas to emphasise.

Vignettes

Vignette is a word often used in home staging. Vignettes are the things that will evoke the emotion you want a buyer to feel. For example, in your favourite book corner, you'll position your chair towards the fireplace. There will be a cosy throw and a cushion to snuggle into. The small table to hand will have a couple of novels stacked next to a fragrant candle and a designer mug ready for coffee. Starting to get the picture? Use objects to emotionally connect your viewers with the best aspects of your home.

You can create as many vignettes as you like, but I suggest sticking to three or four so as not to overdo it. We'll pop a tray with a coffee pot and some biscuits onto a guest bed, and we usually fully lay a dining table as if a dinner party is about to happen. These touches will emphasise lifestyle. If you've lived somewhere for a long time, you'll know what works in your home. The coffee machine in the garage and the road bikes in the barn mentioned earlier are examples of outdoor vignettes. You might ask your children to create one to appeal to the children of any family looking around. A favourite of mine is to set up a train track in a playroom as if the child has left the room for a moment.

Focal point

On a larger scale, when you're tidying and perhaps rearranging your furniture to show a room off to its best, think about the room's focal point – and also the point from which your viewer will first see the room (the doorway), as discussed earlier. If you have multiple doorways into one room, decide on how you or your agent will show people around and use the doorway viewers will use as your point to create your impression.

In general, symmetry is universally accepted as a denominator of beauty. If you can create symmetry in a room, it's more likely to feel beautiful. Symmetry works best around a single focal point. Fireplaces (especially in older houses with alcoves on either side), televisions and bifold doors are all focal points in a sitting room. Your room will feel more pleasing if the furniture faces the fireplace. And placing matching tables with lamps in the alcoves is a simple way to bring a room together. If you have a TV in a sitting room with a fireplace, you may want to move it to a family room or a snug while you're on the market.

If you're marketing your home in the summer and it also has bifold doors to the garden, it may be more appropriate to angle the furniture slightly towards them. You might be able to split larger rooms to use two focal points. This is fine as long as the areas are distinct, separated perhaps by a console table or arranged around a rug in a different colour. In more modern homes, the television is often the focus of a sitting room. The seating is oriented to look at the TV and the placement of furniture is symmetrical as far as possible on each side. If the television is pushed into a corner and the furniture is randomly placed to look vaguely in the direction of that corner, the room won't likely be appealing.

Balance

Once you've decided on your focal point and sorted out the room's symmetry, consider the balance. Balance is about too much or too little on the walls or furniture. Too many cushions and no artwork will push a room out of balance, as will a sideboard laden with ornaments in a room with an empty coffee table.

The rule of three works well to help you balance a room. Remember, groups of objects in odd numbers are more attractive than in even numbers. Try it! You could go for five or even seven objects in a group, as long as it doesn't look like clutter. Three photo frames on a dresser, especially in different shapes or sizes but with similar frames, will look good. Three vases in the same colour but different sizes will work. My top tip is always to take everything off furniture surfaces and put the items on the floor. Choose the things you like best, or most need to keep in the room, and group them into threes with some kind of logic. These are the groups of objects you're going to put back. Everything else can be packed.

While you're thinking about balance, think about connection too. You can connect a room, making it feel like it has been planned as one space, by using the same colour in three different areas. For example, connect the colour in a picture with a cushion and maybe a vase. Then hang a picture or a mirror above a piece of furniture keeping it physically connected to the vase (ie the height of the vase reaches partially over the picture.) If the picture is much higher than the vase, then the three objects will appear to be randomly placed and not part of a well-balanced grouping. Consider height and width. Hanging something too high will look odd. The ideal height for a mirror above a dressing table, for example, is about 15 to 20 cm. And the width of art or a mirror should ideally be about 75% of the width of the piece of furniture it sits above. If your art is small, group frames together gallery style so that you get the proportions right. Your frames don't have to match, nor does all your art have to be the same style. But do try out the gallery you're creating on the floor first. Hanging pictures takes time, and it's much better to practise before banging picture hooks into your walls.

Leave space in your room for your viewers to walk between the furniture. Don't block the walking route or the visual route through the room. This is particularly important if you have a window with a view your potential buyers will want to see, or if they need to walk through one room to get to the next.

A word about flowers before we move on. As a business, we use a lot of faux-flower arrangements in houses we prepare for sale, but only ones where you have to touch them to check if they're real or not. Getting high quality faux-flower arrangements means you don't have to remember, or find time, to buy fresh ones every time you have a viewing. If you prefer fresh and have time, they can look stunning, especially on a well-chosen surface which catches the viewer's eye as they enter a room. Remember, though, that not everyone loves the smell. Lilies are a 'love them or hate them' flower, for example. You don't want to cause your potential buyer to turn down your house because they sneezed the entire way around.

In summary

- Make sure there's a logical flow through the rooms in your home.

- Every room should have a clearly defined purpose and be furnished accordingly.

- If you have a lot of reception rooms or more than four bedrooms, consider giving one of the additional rooms a different purpose to enhance the lifestyle on offer.

- Carefully consider what the outside space could offer.

- Clear garages and outbuildings to show how they could be used as more than a dumping ground.

- Use carefully positioned furniture and accessories to draw attention to your home's best features.

- Create vignettes of your favourite spots in the house.

- Think about symmetry, focal points and balance when arranging your rooms.

- Get rid of the 'visual noise' – aim for a calm flow through your home.

SEVEN

Stage

We always recommend preparing your home for the market before getting photos taken and putting the details on a property portal, for all the reasons discussed in earlier chapters. That said, many homes are on the market for some time before anyone considers the problem their presentation is causing. As a vendor, you may have had viewers tell you that they think your home will be 'too much work'. This is the most common euphemism for 'it's cluttered and badly decorated'. It's easy to become defensive at this stage and wait for the one buyer who loves your style, or can at least see past it sufficiently to make an offer. This may take years.

If there's no serious interest in your home in the first six weeks or so, it's time to take stock. There are a few options.

- **Should you change your estate agent?** This decision will usually depend on whether you feel the agent has been proactive or whether the lack of interest, at least in part, is due to the agent listing the property and then sitting back and waiting for buyers to come along.

- **Should you drop the price?** The estate agent will likely suggest this. It's always an interesting conversation. 'Well if it isn't worth that much now, why did you list it at that in the first place?' against 'You wanted me to list it high, saying you're not in a rush. I did explain that the guide price was aspirational.' It's often difficult to work out whether an agent has been overambitious in their valuation or whether they've felt pressured by a vendor to list high to get the instruction. Be honest with yourself as the vendor. Did you pressure your agent to put your property onto the market at a valuation they described as 'hopeful'? If so, now is the time to listen to more realistic advice.

- **Or should you take a serious look at your home's presentation?** Did you launch before addressing the outstanding issues you were hoping you wouldn't have to spend any time or money on? If so, now is the time to address them. It's entirely possible that changing the presentation will make enough difference and you won't need to change the price at all.

Stage or drop?

If you're planning to drop your price, you may want to consider this advice from Sam Ashdown, who works as an adviser to many estate agents: 'DON'T drop your asking price by less than 10%.'[20]

Her view is that you won't significantly increase the interest you get from potential buyers who will usually look at properties 10% above the value they can afford anyway. And 10% of any guide price will buy an awful lot of staging. It's definitely worth investing just a tenth of that amount of a proposed drop in price in serious reconsideration of the presentation before taking the hit on price.

It's also important to know how property portals group guide prices. If your home is on the market at less than £300,000, you'll only need to drop your price by £10,000 to drop into the next price bracket and perhaps attract a different group of potential buyers. As the guide price goes up, so too do the price bands. Once your guide price is £800,000, you'll need to drop £100,000 to reach anyone searching in a different price band. We also know agents who will recommend a £5 price increase on a property that is listed at £499,995 to take it to £500,000. This ensures it's one of the first properties that appears on the screen of someone searching for a property up to £500,000.

---

20 www.home-truths.co.uk/dos-donts-dropping-asking-price-house
-wont-sell

How do the numbers stack up?

Deciding whether to stage your property is difficult from a financial perspective. A confident property stager might say that it will cost 1% or 2% of your guide price to do the work to significantly improve your presentation. The first price drop that an agent suggests is usually around 5%. From this stance, it seems like a no-brainer. Why wouldn't you go for the 2% option rather than the 5% option?

It has taken me a long time in the business to even begin to understand the thinking that allows a vendor to say to me, 'Elaine, I understand what you're saying and I know the numbers should convince me, but I think I'll go for dropping my price instead.' Every time this happens, the mathematical part of my brain screams NO and my team have to go out and fetch cake and make coffee to calm me down. On a logical level, I'll never understand this approach, but I have learned a lot about what underlies this thinking.

Sometimes the decision to drop rather than stage is a simple matter of cash flow. For many vendors, cash is tight before a property sale. This is particularly true in the case of a family selling an inherited house and the case of separations or divorces. The financial aspect at this stage is important, but many staging companies offer the option to pay on completion of the sale. They may not advertise this because it impacts their own cash flow, but if you ask, they may well agree.

Let's assume that your agent got the valuation of your home right in the first instance. One reason people will choose to drop the price rather than stage the property is that the costs of staging are 'real' and the cost of dropping isn't. Staging comes with immediate costs: engaging professional help, decorating materials, accessories, storage space, etc. The cost of dropping the price doesn't have an invoice attached. It's theoretical money, so its impact won't be felt until it influences what you're able to buy post-sale.

As well, the changes involved in staging the property will inevitably impact your day-to-day life. The house will look and feel different. Treasures that have cluttered the living space for many years will need to be moved. Memories might surface in the process, and you'll have to make difficult decisions about whether to pack items for the move or send them to a new home. You may also need to allow strangers to help with the decluttering or to bring in additional furniture. The psychological aspect of sorting out and starting to let go of the life you've had in a house can be tough. It's easy to see why the more passive decision, 'just drop the price', is so often made.

Many vendors will argue that there are no guarantees that dressing a property will attract a buyer. That, of course, is completely true. Equally, neither does a price drop guarantee a buyer. Unless, of course, the price drop is huge. Many agents will tell you, based on the evidence they've seen over the last few years, that if a lack of ability to visualise the lifestyle a property offers is actually the problem, dropping the price won't be the answer. Buyers would rather wait for something new to come to the market than spend their precious money on a property they aren't in love with, however cheap it is.

A word of advice: don't expect that you'll be able to increase the price of your home once it has been staged. The staging is meant to improve the presentation at the current price. It's aimed at increasing saleability, not value.

Right price + great presentation = quick sale

BE REALISTIC

We saw a good example of this in a beautiful Victorian home. The vendors had moved out already, leaving the house empty. We worked closely with a premium agent who gives excellent advice. He explained to the vendors that once the property was fully furnished and some of the more glaring repairs had been done, the house should be returned to the market at its original guide price. The vendors insisted that it go back on for a higher price to reflect the money they'd spent on staging. Unfortunately, the house got stuck again. It was now on the market for too much money. The vendor sacked the agent and everyone was hugely frustrated.

CASE STUDY

I used the data we collect from every property we dress to explain to a vendor why dropping her price wasn't a good idea.

Potential outcome if you drop the price
Original guide price: £750,000
Drop to next search bracket: £50,000
Percentage drop: 6.7%
New guide price: £700,000
Time on the market: 161 days
Likely accepted offer: £685,000
Selling price vs guide: 91%

Potential outcome if you stage the house
Original guide price: £750,000
Cost of staging: £7,500
Percentage cost of staging: 1%
Time on the market: 44 days
Likely accepted offer: £735,000
Selling price vs guide: 97% (including dressing)

These statistics were taken from our 2018/2019 figures of lived-in properties which had been listed on the market before we staged.

A DIFFERENT OPINION

A sale that led to the recruitment of the agent onto my team was that of a property situated in a lovely village near Ashbourne, in Derbyshire. It had been newly renovated with six gorgeous bedrooms and offered stunning views over the surrounding countryside.

The property had been on the market for around a year with no interest before we were asked to take a look.

Due to the renovation and the vendors' subsequent relocation, the property lacked a lived-in feel. All the walls were painted white, there were no pictures or mirrors and furniture was minimal. We explained to the vendors that it can be hard for prospective buyers to visualise themselves living in such a large property and to work out the purpose of each room unless it's fully furnished.

Since the property had been stuck for a while, the vendor invited four agents, including the one who already had it on the market, to comment on the reasons for the property not selling. All but one recommended a significant price drop, varying from 6% to 12%. The fourth suggested that we get involved and leave the price untouched. This was the option the vendor decided to go for.

We reorganised the layout using our furniture to ensure the house flowed correctly and each room had a purpose. We also rented some additional furniture, pictures and accessories to complement what the vendors already owned, and new professional marketing photos were taken. Our costs to change the presentation and add some furniture, artwork and accessories came to about 1% of the guide price. The house returned to the market with no change to the guide price and an offer was accepted within six weeks. No price drop was necessary – simply much better presentation.

We have so many similar stories of successful interventions. It most certainly isn't luck or coincidence when changing the presentation initiates a sale where interest has been lacking.

Something important to keep in mind: the way the property portals work will influence whether you decide to come off the market while any work is done. Rightmove and Zoopla have rules about how long your property must be offline if it's to be relaunched as a new listing. There are also rules about how big the price drop must be in order for it to appear at the top of the listings as a price reduction. Ask your agent which packages they have on the portals and what the rules are. You may be able to come off the market, change your presentation and go back online as a premium listing. Some agents offer 'premium listing' as part of their marketing package; some ask vendors to pay extra for it. If you can relaunch to the market as a new or premium listing, your new photos are more likely to attract attention from prospective buyers who haven't yet seen them. This is worth thinking about, even if it means you need to wait an extra couple of weeks.

Empty properties

So far we have mostly been discussing occupied properties which are already furnished. We've talked about decluttering and decorating and changing the flow and functionality of rooms using existing furniture. But what happens if you've already moved out of your home and left it empty?

An empty property can inadvertently convey the message that the vendor is desperate to sell. While the house may attract offers, these are likely to be well below any guide price. It's clear to anyone looking that if a house is empty, the vendor has already moved on. Many people will assume that this is because they have moved to a different area. Having to keep visiting a house at a distance is a hassle, so potential buyers may believe the vendor will want to get rid of the house quickly. Alternatively, the message is that someone has died recently. The family may be assumed to be bearing the costs of an unwanted home and therefore willing to accept a low offer. It's probably clear to you now that selling your home is much more a psychological game than a trading of bricks and mortar. The advantage of knowing this and being willing to play to win is that the game has simple rules and a clearly defined prize. Remember that the best outcomes are those which create a win-win-win situation for you, your agent and your buyer.

To understand why empty properties should be furnished, it's important to know how developers work. Developers build homes as products – they have no emotional attachment to them as the places where they live or have lived. There's a good reason why all the big house builders create show homes almost as soon as the first house on the development is completed. They need viewers to fall in love with the development so that all the homes sell well.

In the Home Staging Association's 2019 report, 100% of developers said that the properties they staged sold faster than the non-staged ones and 83% of them also recognised an increase in the property value as a result of the staging.[21]

Financially, developers need to get early reservations on as many of the homes that aren't yet built as they possibly can. This gives them the cash flow to carry on building and to keep their financiers happy. They have learned that the best way to attract commitment from potential buyers is to showcase the lifestyle that living on the development will offer. Individual vendors can learn a lot from the bigger developers' marketing strategies, even though lived-in properties may be quirkier and the space more difficult to stage.

Developers understand that it's almost impossible to photograph empty rooms and use the resulting photos or videos to attract anyone to view. One neutral colour wall and carpet looks much like another. As we saw in Chapter One, buyers of the Instagram generation are used to looking at beautiful images of carefully curated interiors. They won't be remotely interested in having to do the hard work of imagining themselves living in what they're currently seeing as an empty house.

---

21 Home Staging Association of UK and Ireland Report 2019,
    www.homestaging.org.uk

I'm astonished every time a vendor is prepared to put an empty home on the market. It strikes me as being akin to a luxury-car manufacturer building cars quietly in their factory and then expecting people to buy them with no advertising, no imagery of the lifestyle the car offers – just an expectation that people will find the cars and buy them because they're nice. Vendors will say to me, 'Well, it's the estate agent's job to sell the house.' A vendor can help their estate agent or hinder them. Giving the agent an empty home to sell is a hindrance not a help. Giving them a fully furnished, beautifully presented home that photographs well will allow the agent to prepare a top-quality brochure and online presence to attract buyers quickly.

It's also difficult to gauge the size of rooms if there's no furniture. One of the most important questions a viewer has in mind is 'Will my furniture fit?' Bedrooms are notorious for appearing much smaller than they are if there's no bed. Many times we've been able to demonstrate a room's ability to accommodate a full-sized double bed where multiple viewers thought a single was the only option.

A SIMPLE FIX

In one case, a three-bedroom property, there was a double bed in one room, a single in another and nothing at all in the third. The agent asked if I would pop out to the house and shed some light on why it wasn't selling. On my visit, a free consultation, I simply moved the single bed into the third bedroom, which was the smallest and looked as though a bed might not fit at all. The next viewer bought the house!

Virtual staging

We're often asked whether we think it's better to stage a house virtually than to move in real furniture for the time it's on the market. There are some good companies offering virtual staging and CGI graphics for the property market, and staging a house this way is considerably less expensive than using real furniture. Developers can really benefit from using CGI images. They can create beautiful interiors before the actual house has come out of the ground. This will draw in those buyers who are happy to buy a property off-plan or generate interest in the site so that the moment the show home is ready, people are queuing up to view. We may also recommend CGI images for rental property that's being let unfurnished. It's a relatively inexpensive option for a landlord and the images can be kept and reused each time the apartment needs a new tenant.

That said, my answer to the question is almost always no, virtual staging is often not enough. The reason I'm not a fan of using virtual staging in a completed property goes back to the fact that buying a house is an emotional decision. Great imagery will attract buyers to view. Because of the high quality of some of these images, it can be hard to tell if the furniture is real or not. This means that viewers may arrive at a property they have fallen in love with online – they haven't fallen in love with the walls and the floors but the lifestyle the furniture in the photos creates. As soon as the door is opened, they can see there's no furniture. And the first emotion will be disappointment. They'll spend the rest of the viewing feeling cheated, either at a conscious or a subconscious level, of the life they envisioned themselves living in this house. It would be rare for a viewer to then make an offer for that property, and if they were still willing to do so, it would be made from their logical brain, not their emotional brain. The logical brain always makes lower offers than the emotional brain. So, if a house hasn't sold off-plan with virtually staged images, put the real furniture in before viewings commence.

THE REAL DEAL

One of our lovely developers, someone for whom we had dressed a lot of properties in the past, had a single house remaining on a small development he'd done. He was frustrated because it hadn't sold and he was already coming to the end of his next site. The house needed to go. He changed agents, and his new agent asked him why he hadn't asked us to furnish it. He replied that he didn't really want the expense and he thought the next step would be to get some CGI images done. She tried to persuade him otherwise, but he went ahead and remarketed the house anyway. It attracted no offers in the next four-month period, although the images created a lot more interest. Eventually he gave in and called me to see how quickly we could fully furnish it for him. Within two weeks of this furnishing, he had his buyer!

Having said that, virtual staging became a lifeline for many properties during the COVID-19 crisis. So many vendors found themselves with empty properties on the market. And suddenly there were far more people at home with time to look at new homes. We staged a lot of homes virtually to attract as much interest as possible once the market began to move again.

In summary

- Stage your home before your marketing begins to achieve your quickest sale.

- If you didn't stage at the outset and are stuck, come off the market and do so now.

- Give serious consideration to staging your home rather than dropping the price, taking any feedback into account.

- Don't market your property when it's empty. Hire or buy furniture to place in every room. It will photograph much better and attract more viewings.

- Buying a home is an emotional decision, and it's hard to fall in love with empty rooms.

We've completed the first six stages of our ADDRESS system. Now it's time to look at the final stage: Sell. But first, some tips for living in a staged home.

EIGHT

Living In A Staged Home Until You Sell

I put off starting this chapter, and it ended up being the last one I wrote. I was worried it might be a bit dry and become a list of tasks: put things into boxes, find cupboard space, etc. Then one day I came across a list of Old English words that have largely gone out of fashion. In among *squizzle* and *chaddy*, *curflag* and *jirging* and, of course, pettifogging, I came across the verb *scurryfunge*. What a lovely term! And it's perfect for anyone who has their home on the market. To scurryfunge is 'to rush around the house tidying in the time one sees a neighbour leaving their own house approaching your house'![22] Apparently, the word fell

---

22 www.collinsdictionary.com/submission/20717/Scurryfunge

out of the English dictionary around 1882 but has recently been submitted for readmission.[23] I would certainly support that, with a slight amendment to the definition:

> Scurryfunge – 'To rush around the house shoving things into cupboards and under the beds in the hour between the estate agent phoning and the viewer arriving.'

So the alternative title of this chapter is 'Top Tips for an Efficient Scurryfunge.'

Mind the gap

At this stage, you've put an enormous amount of work into getting your home ready to sell. You have, assuming you used the model, assessed the problem, the competition and your likely buyer. You have decluttered and decluttered again. You've had decorators painting over any dated colours and touching up the bashed skirtings and bannisters. You have re-imagined your rooms into spaces that have more universal appeal, emphasised the best features of your home and staged ahead of the photographer arriving. Now you're ready to sell.

---

23 Kacirk, J, *Forgotten English* (William Morrow Paperbacks, 1997)

This is sometimes the moment when our clients fall in love with their own houses all over again.

A CHANGE OF HEART

I clearly remember the frustration of one agent. A £2 million property was coming onto the market, and he was already lining up prospective buyers. We worked with the owners to make the house look worthy of the price tag. We tidied the three teenage children and the two dogs into submission and relocated the dining table into the TV area, to the father's huge chagrin. We cleaned and brought in accessories to complement the family's furniture. They held an open day at the estate agent's instigation and the next day, having received many compliments about the house and the information that someone was ready to make an offer, they withdrew from the market. They decided that the house was perfect for family occasions and that they would rent a place when they relocated for work. I had to make my peace with the estate agent on that occasion.

Usually what happens, though, is that the moment the photographer closes the door behind them, you breathe a huge sigh of relief. The kids let out whoops of joy, and toys and books they haven't been allowed to play with for weeks are emptied onto the sitting room floor. The dog rushes in from the garden covered in mud, wagging his tail against the sparkling cupboard doors and walking his muddy paws over the lately polished tiles. Aaaargh! This is the moment to 'mind the gap'. Don't let things get out of control now, or you'll have more work to do all over again in a week or two.

'The gap' is how we refer to the short hiatus, a few days, perhaps, while your agent does their bit. Your photos will be added to your marketing details and launched onto the internet portals. You should expect professional photos to be turned around in forty-eight hours. Your photographer will pick out the best angles, make a few tweaks and transfer them to your agent. Your agent will then select the ones to be used for both the online marketing and for your brochure, if you're having one. Accepted wisdom seems to be that one photo isn't enough and thirty is too many. Our advice is to use between twelve and fifteen good images online. You're tempting anyone looking for a new home in your area to come and view, not trying to show them absolutely everything at this stage. The key areas to show in photos are the kitchen/living area, sitting room, main bedroom and the most impressive bathroom. You will also want to show off any other areas you think are especially appealing (remember those carefully created vignettes?). Seduce your potential buyer to come and look in person. Whet their appetite. Show them too much and they may just flick past, thinking they've seen everything.

Once you've officially launched, potential buyers will be able to look at your photos and videos online, contact your agent and book a viewing. A wise vendor will use the time between when the photos are taken and the viewings start to work out the least stressful ways to keep the house immaculate for the weeks until a sale is secured. A good home staging company will have left you with advice about how to make this easy and with offers to return to help at critical moments.

Living in the 'show house'– minimal work, maximum impact

My all-time top tip: get plastic lidded boxes, lots of them, in different colours and issued to all members of the house, including the pets. I'm sure the use of plastic boxes doesn't fit well with climate-change prevention measures, but sadly, cardboard will prove woefully inadequate. And remember, we're trying to minimise your stress levels. The plastic boxes will be able to be repurposed post-move and certainly won't be thrown away.

Your major decluttering has been done by this point, and family treasures, possessions in excess of imme-diate need and possibly a few things you actually did need have been consigned to storage, even if that's only the garage. (Remember, when decluttering, be careful to hold on to the things you might need before the move, and if someone is helping you declutter, put precious belongings to one side first.)

CASE OF THE MISSING RETAINER

As I sat down to watch *Silent Witness* one evening after a busy day, the phone rang. It was Jill, the client my team had been working alongside all day. We were helping to declutter her home.

> 'Um, Elaine, I don't suppose you thought to put my daughter's retainer somewhere obvious when you decluttered, did you?'

> 'Well, where was it?'

> 'On the windowsill above the kitchen sink.'

> 'Have a look in the cupboard under the sink then.'

Fortunately, that was where it had been moved to ahead of the photographer arriving. Small but important items are easy to lose in a big declutter, especially if the photographer's arrival is imminent. Hang on to things like retainers, TV remotes and vital lists.

But there's almost always day-to-day clutter to deal with (unless, as a family, you're unusual). Loose change, wallets and phones tend to land on the first table in the hall. School bags are dumped in the hallway and crumbs left on the chopping board in the kitchen. Bathrooms are clutter magnets, attracting half-squeezed tubes of toothpaste, loose bottle caps and damp towels. Dirty washing piles up on bedroom floors or in front of the washing machine, and leaves rush in every time the front door is opened. All this detritus adds to the length of time it takes to scurryfunge ahead of a viewing. You can help the situation by leaving lidded boxes in each area where clutter is likely to accumulate. Place small ones on top of furniture where keys and change are likely to be deposited. Use larger ones in bathrooms and bedrooms for everything that would otherwise be stored on the floor. Bedspread, throw and cushions will come out of the bedroom's viewing kit, towels and toiletries out of the bathroom's – and in goes the clutter. With good organisation, this will take ten minutes, not two hours (in which you have to iron clean linen and search for a space in a cupboard to stuff the shampoo).

The final magic happens when you remember that, as part of the original decluttering programme, you created space in the bottom of the wardrobe for hiding away the plastic boxes. Hiding the boxes is often the biggest concern many of our clients have.

TEMPORARY FIXES

We worked with a young couple selling a sweet but tiny cottage. The house's internal storage capacity was no longer sufficient for their needs and they couldn't put anything into longer-term storage because most things were necessary on a day-to-day basis. Every time they had a viewing (fortunately there were only three or four before they accepted an offer), poor Simon had to load the boxes into the back of his car and then park the car around the corner. The car, your neighbour's garage and the garden shed are all options.

The big clean

The final step in preparing for viewings is known in our office as 'the big clean'. Happily, unless a house is very dirty, the need for cleaning doesn't show in photos. Carpets may well have to be cleaned ahead of any staging, especially if furniture is to be changed. It's much easier to professionally clean carpets while rooms are empty. Likewise, if any decorating has been done, the newly decorated rooms will have been cleaned before the furniture was returned. The final-sparkle clean, though, can be done in the period between your photos being taken and your viewers arriving. If you're using a professional team, book them well in advance. Like any other professionals, the good ones are always busy.

Don't forget to book the window cleaner at this stage as well. Many photographers will take the interior shots on a day when it isn't too bright outside. It helps ensure that there are no big shadows and the light from the windows doesn't make your rooms appear overexposed. But windows will always appear dirty on a sunny day unless they're freshly cleaned, and you may have viewers on a sunny day. Tackle this problem before anyone arrives.

As we've chatted about, the kitchen is one of the most important rooms to consider when you're selling. It must be absolutely spotless. Take out pet food, litter trays and all bins ahead of viewings. Even if you've just had a big clean done, go around with the cleaning spray and wipe everything again. Do the same with your bathrooms. Any areas where you use water are in danger of acquiring a smell. Even water that has been on the side of the sink for a while has a smell. Keep a cloth handy and swipe all wet areas in your scurryfunge moment.

Don't forget to look under the furniture. We've found takeaway pizza boxes with the last piece of pizza being used as an experiment in growing penicillin, sweaty gym kit ready to crawl to the washing machine all by itself and piles of adult magazines under beds. All these things will put your viewers off should they notice them – they don't represent a lifestyle they'll want to buy into. You may well have dealt with these things during the declutter phase; this is the time to check and check again that nothing unsavoury has worked its way back into the house while you had your back turned.

Finally, remember the importance of smell (see Chapter Four). Smells are powerful – people remember them. They can instantly transport us to a happy memory. I only have to get the faintest whiff of a warm acacia bush to be in my twenties and loving life working in Greece. Use this sense to your advantage. Help your viewers remember your home by its great smell.

Quick tips and reminders:

- Open all the windows ahead of your viewings for a few minutes. Even in winter. Nothing makes a house smell fresh more quickly than letting the outside in. The only time to perhaps reconsider this step is if the wind is blowing 40 knots and the rain is torrential.

- Use a luxurious diffuser on each floor of the house (a consistent smell is like a consistent colour theme – calming).

- Pop a few coffee beans into a pan on the stove and roast gently, or make fresh coffee if you have time.

- Sprinkle a fresh loaf of bread (doesn't have to be homemade but doesn't work well with a sliced loaf in a plastic packet) with a little water and put into a hot oven or the microwave for a few moments. You can create the smell of a freshly baked loaf without having to do the hard work of actually baking one.

Pets

We're often asked, 'What do I do with pets and evidence of pets?' Unfortunately, there's no easy answer. The main problem is the smell that having pets in the house generates. We've spoken already about getting carpets cleaned, especially if you have dogs, and about the need to consider pets at the decluttering stage.

If possible, let animals go outside into the garden or for a play date with a neighbour while there's a viewing. Their bedding should be washed regularly, or relegated to the garage, and litter trays and food should be moved out of any living areas. Remember, even pet lovers are put off by the presence of other people's pets. And some pets are scary. We've worked in homes where the children kept rats and, worse still, tarantulas as pets. Many viewers will remember a house where these creatures are residents for all the wrong reasons. If you're serious about selling, you may need to find them temporary new homes for the duration of your being on the market.

Packing for your move

You may have started packing as part of your declutter process. Or you may have shoved everything into cupboards and piled things into the garage so you could get onto the market as quickly as possible. Now is the time to get ahead for the next stage of your move. Top tip: decide on your removal company early. Get a quote. Once you've accepted it, the company will be able to drop off packing boxes for you. They usually don't charge for these if they're going to do your removal. If you're not ready to make that decision yet, Amazon has a range of boxes in different sizes. Do buy the strong ones, even though they're more expensive. I still have nightmares of crossing the road with a clients' books and the bottom falling out of the box they were in.

There's something deeply horrifying about the thud twenty large volumes make as they hit the tarmac on a busy road.

Also buy permanent markers and packing tape. Double the quantity you think you'll need. I promise you'll use it all. Mark all the boxes with both the room the items have come from and also the piece of furniture in which the items were stored. It's much easier to have extra boxes all partly full than putting everything from one room into a single box. Unpacking will be much quicker if you know which box belongs with which piece of furniture. We believe in this methodology so deeply that we do it for all our staging furniture too. A bookshelf will travel with its own accessory box, and woe betide any new team member who tries to change the box's contents.

A removal company will also be able to bring you some clothes rails – usually cardboard boxes with a rail inside so that you can simply move your wardrobes into boxes without having to fold items. Of course, you may not want to store your clothes ahead of your move, but if you're selling in the spring, it may be convenient to put your winter clothes on rails ready to go to their new home rather than leave them cluttering the wardrobe. As mentioned, you need space for your scurryfunge boxes, and you need to help your viewers believe that your home has more than sufficient storage. This is an illusion you can create by ensuring all the storage areas are two-thirds full at most.

Storage pre-move

Where to store everything once it has been packed ready to move? Many removal companies have links with a storage facility and may even be able to offer you a preferential rate if they're doing your move. There are multiple storage facilities around, and it's well worth shopping around for the best rate – there are big differences. Make sure that the space you choose is accessible, preferably with twenty-four-hour access. You'll have peace of mind knowing that if you have an urgent need for a cocktail dress when you thought the dress code was smart casual, you can fetch your favourite LBD from the facility. Again, make sure you label your boxes effectively. It's worth writing on at least two sides in permanent marker in case the box is moved. Sticky labels will get knocked off or the glue will get old and fail before you move everything out of storage. There's nothing more frustrating than having to open every single box to find the one thing you need.

You may have a garage or other building to house your belongings until your move. At one house we decluttered, I was outside unloading some accessories and a neighbour of our client came over and offered help. I said, 'The only help we need right now is someone with a large empty garage.' Immediately she offered her own and even carried boxes to it – a great lesson in asking for what you want and tapping into resources you didn't know were available.

In summary

- Be careful that the house doesn't revert to normal after all your hard work tidying and cleaning in the gap that occurs between the photographs being taken and your viewings starting.

- You can do a deep clean after your photos have been done. Unless it's very dirty, the house's cleanliness won't impact your photos. But a home that feels clean to viewers actually inside it will keep them looking for longer. The viewer who rushes off quickly because they can't stand the smell isn't going to be your buyer.

- Equip every family member with a big, lidded box and have smaller boxes around the house. These boxes are your secret to a successful scurryfunge before a viewing.

- Find storage for any large items or boxes away from your home so they don't clutter the garage or the cupboards.

NINE

Sell

As we've talked about, selling a house is like any other major life event: it takes planning and time to get it right. The whole process will be much more straightforward if you have the right team helping you. It's worth spending time doing your research and thinking through what you'll need before you start. This chapter sets out a guide to the people who can help you and the questions you might want to ask before recruiting them. There are plenty of frustrations inherent in selling a house. Knowing you have a professional, competent team to whom you can turn for speedy solutions will make all the difference in overcoming the frustrations and moving forward.

I suggest building a team that consists of an agent, a solicitor, a home stager and a professional photographer. Your agent may be able to recommend the other

SELL HIGH, SELL FAST

team members, but if you're not entirely happy with the recommendations, don't be afraid to ask for advice from others until you find the people you think you can work with. The whole process, from start to finish, may take up to six months – you need people you can trust to do their best for you.

Choosing your agent – online vs high street vs national

There are big differences in agents these days, and one of the first decisions you'll need to make is whether to use a traditional/high street agent or an online agent. Before choosing one, spend a few minutes answering this question for yourself: 'What do I expect my agent to do for me?' It isn't enough to simply expect them to sell your home. Think about the balance of your time against the costs you want to pay.

How do you shop?

- Where do you buy your groceries? Aldi, Waitrose or the independent stores on your village's high street?

- Where do you go for your new clothes? Primark, John Lewis or the designer stores on Bond Street?

- Do you do all your shopping online, preferring the anonymity and convenience of the service?

With your shopping preferences in mind, consider how you want to sell your house – through Purplebricks, a local agent with a strong reputation or one of the high-end national agents? Your choice will also depend on the style of house you're selling. As one agent said to me recently, 'If I'm going to value a manor house in the hope of getting the instruction to sell, I'll take examples of manor houses we have sold recently.' People like to see direct comparisons with their own situation. An early client of mine told me that, although a friend of his had recommended our services, he almost didn't call because there were no examples of huge Georgian rectories on our website, which was the style of home he was wanting to sell. Ironically, after we worked with him to get his house ready for sale, we went through a few months where we seemed to stage only Georgian rectories!

A whole field of psychology is dedicated to how we shop and how products and services can be marketed as a result. It's big business. My point is to ask yourself, 'When I shop, what's most important to me?' For example, wild horses couldn't drag me into any store which doesn't have rails organised according to size and colour. I know many of them have fantastic deals and products, but these stores vividly remind me of the weekly jumble sale in the community hall near where I grew up. People would jostle for bargains, elbows and sharp tongues at the ready. I know I probably pay more for a similar look, but I love the calm stores, clothes set out on rails with plenty of space between and my posh coffee to fire up my shopping head.

Think about what you're asking of your agent and their marketing before you decide whom to instruct. Let's go back to our win-win-win scenario. If you pay a minimal fee, you'll probably need to do much of the work. You may need to conduct your own viewings, and you won't get professional photography or a glossy brochure. Once you have accepted an offer, be clear about who will do the progression of the sale. There's a lot of time and effort to be invested in following the progression of your sale with the chasing solicitors, ensuring funds are available and complying with all the money laundering legislation. If you're choosing to do the progression yourself because you want to save on the commission fee, be clear about the amount of time this is likely to take and the fact that it probably isn't your area of expertise.

Speeding up your sale post-offer – the right solicitor

Which? online reported that a quarter of prospective home sales fell through in 2019. The main reasons for this were mortgage issues, broken chains and gazumping.[24] While having the right solicitor working for you

---

24 www.which.co.uk/news/2020/01/five-reasons-house-sales-fall -through-and-how-to-avoid-them

can't completely remove the risk of any of these things becoming a problem, in my experience of buying and selling, a good solicitor is worth their weight in gold. They'll flag issues before they become deal-breakers, usually with a workable solution to hand. Many properties get stuck at this stage with each side blaming each other for delays. And delays can cause your buyer to pull out and look for another property. Choosing the right legal team can make a huge difference to the speed of your sale. Don't give your buyer time to get cold feet or become frustrated with the process.

A few questions to consider before you appoint your legal representative:

- Do you need a solicitor or a conveyancer?

- Are you buying as well as selling?

- What is the value of the home you're selling/ buying?

- Is it a standard property type or a one-off?

- Are there complex covenants on your title deed?

Inevitably, some sales fall through, so when getting a quote, it's worthwhile seeing if your solicitor or conveyancer can offer a 'no sale, no fee' deal to shield yourself from being out of pocket. That said, most conveyancers and solicitors will ask for some upfront costs to cover their initial disbursements, such as searches. They will have had to conduct these whether your sale goes ahead or not and will have had to pay for them themselves.

Again, do your homework, get more than one recommendation, get quotes, check review sites and speak to anyone you're planning to appoint to ensure you're confident they can deliver what you need – before you pay anything.

Referrals

Estate agents will often recommend a conveyancer or a solicitor to you. They may do so through an incentivised selling and conveyancing package, or they may refer you to a conveyancer with whom they have a commercial relationship. They are obliged by law to disclose any referral fees that pass between them as a result of referring your business. The commercial partnerships that your agent has may be useful for you – they will have worked with many of the solicitors and other professionals involved in buying and selling homes for many years and will know who is good at their job. It's in your estate agent's best interests for your sale to progress quickly. If you're using a traditional agent or a 'no sale, no fee' package from an online agent, the agent won't be getting paid until your sale is complete. But be wary of recommendations from any agent you have paid ahead of completion – they don't have such a vested interest in your sale going through quickly, and an unscrupulous agent may recommend only on the basis of their referral fee. You are entitled to ask for this information, and it must be disclosed to you.

Choosing a professional property stager

In earlier chapters, we looked at the difference property staging can make to your sale. Choosing a professional property stager to help you can be difficult in the UK, as the concept of staging for sale is relatively new, but your estate agent may be able to recommend a good local business.

If you're searching online, Home Staging Association UK and Ireland, a membership organisation for home staging professionals, is a good place to start. Businesses are organised according to the geographic locations they cover. After you have found some options in your area, have a good look at the websites. Remember, this will be the team you trust to prepare your home to look its absolute best for marketing. Do their photos reflect the look you want? If you're happy at this stage, here are some questions you may want to ask on the phone before you invite them to your home to see how they can help.

How long have you been in business?

Do you belong to any professional association? In the UK, this is likely to be the Home Staging Association of UK and Ireland.

How do you charge? This may be by the hour, per project or linked to property value. They may charge upfront or on completion of the sale. This should be clear, and if they work on an hourly rate, you'll want an estimate of the time involved.

How did you get into staging? You should expect some background in property; remember, staging is a property marketing tool, not a branch of interior design.

What training or accreditations do you hold? There are training courses for home staging professionals and the HSA is launching an accreditation programme in late 2020 which will accredit stagers according to their training, experience and results.

What type of projects do you do? As a vendor, you want to know that someone has experience with your type of project. For example, if you need a lot of decluttering, you don't want them to evidence furnishing only new builds. If you have a Victorian manor house stuffed with antiques, you don't want them to more generally work with small new builds furnished with flat-pack furniture.

Could you please show me some case studies of properties like mine? An experienced stager will know that their strongest marketing tools are their case studies and the statistical evidence they have collected from the work they've done. They should be prepared to share all of this with you.

What's the average value of the properties you stage? If you're selling a multi-million-pound property, you need to trust someone to handle a project in a property of this value. If they generally work at the lower end of the market, they're probably not for you. The staging needs to match the property value.

Which agents do you work with? Not all stagers work through estate agents, but if they come recommended by more than one agent, that's a good start.

What's your lead time for a project? I would expect a maximum of two weeks from confirmation of quote unless there's major decorating to be done. Neither vendor nor agent will want to wait for a stager to source the perfect sofa!

Could you explain your process for preparing a property for sale? The process needs to be clear and focused on maximising the sale price. A good stager should be able to source decorators, general maintenance contractors, gardeners, etc. quickly so that nothing delays getting the property onto the market.

How do you evidence the success of your projects? You want to know that they use statistics and data from their own portfolio, not generic and not simply qualitative data.

What else can you do to make my move easier? Could be anything from sourcing a removal team to recommending storage facilities to moving you into your new home by unpacking boxes and placing items within forty-eight hours of the move.

Professional photography

According to the Home Staging Association's 2019 report, '100% of estate agents say properties with professional photographs get more viewings.'[25]

We have established that great images of your home – images which emphasise its features and the lifestyle it offers – are key in attracting buyers. Buying a home is an emotive process. Many people look at Rightmove in the evening, right after looking at their social media accounts, and often not because they're planning to move. Sometimes they'll look for inspiration, sometimes for aspiration, but a lot of the time, it's because humans are naturally voyeuristic. We like to see how other people live and compare our own homes.

One of the aims of amazing property presentation and fabulous photography is to create a market, not just capture the market that already exists. It serves to generate interest in your home not only from the people who are moving but also those who are looking with no intention of buying. The idea is that the photography

---

25 Home Staging Association of UK and Ireland Report 2019, www.homestaging.org.uk

will make them form an emotional attachment to the property because of how it has been presented and photographed. They might then decide to move after all.

Not only do properties with great photos get more viewings, they can also help achieve a faster sale.[26] Unfortunately, justifying the upfront cost to the agent and the home seller can prove difficult. Thankfully, this is beginning to change because of growing awareness of all the help on offer when preparing a home for sale.

It's worth hiring a professional property photographer because they will:

- Take time to get the correct shot

- See through the camera lens anything that needs to be moved, tweaked or fluffed

- Take several angles of each key room, create ambience, light correctly and showcase features

- Edit the shots, not just upload them straight from their camera

- Achieve perfect verticals

- Balance the colour casts in the room

- Add that beautiful blue sky and light the log burner

---

26 www.rismedia.com/2018/12/12/shocking-stats-importance
-photography-real-estate

You hire an agent based on their ability to bring your house to the market and sell your home. Agents are not photographers. You might decide to commission your own photographs from a recommendation. This is fine, and you'll have the advantage of owning the photos rather than your agent owning them. And if you change agents, you won't need to have new photos taken. There may be a higher cost in doing your photos this way – it's worth finding out. A word of warning: don't choose a property photographer based on the evidence of the beautiful wedding photos they took.

The need for a professionally produced video or virtual tour has also increased following the pandemic. Many vendors found themselves on the market with no way of showing prospective buyers around their home when the housing market went into lockdown. Once viewings were allowed to happen again, in many cases videos and virtual tours have been used in place of a first viewing with vendors being reluctant to show all but seriously interested buyers into their homes in person. It is likely that this trend will become the 'new normal'. Once again, a strong argument for ensuring your home is beautifully presented and fully furnished.

A DIFFERENT KIND OF PROFESSIONAL

We once worked with a developer who insisted on using a professional photographer he knew. Sure enough, the photographer was a professional: he took amazing photos of events and weddings. He found it impossible to deal with the curved walls a wide-angle lens can produce. Even though I'd worked in the house, I was convinced by his photos that one of the bathrooms had curved walls.

In summary

- Everyone on your team needs to be experienced in selling property like yours. Ask for evidence.

- Estate agent – Don't go for the cheapest agent giving you the highest valuation. Take time to consider exactly what you expect of them and ask lots of questions about their track record.

- Solicitor or conveyancer – Choose your solicitor before you receive any offers. Make sure they will progress your sale quickly and that they will do a thorough job. Don't choose based on price, or necessarily the one the estate agent recommends. Ask for personal recommendations and check their experience. You may want to use review sites, such as Trustpilot (www.uk.trustpilot.com).

- Consider using a professional home staging company. Ask for case studies of where they have helped sales in your home's price bracket.

- It's always worth the investment to get professional photos and a video done for your marketing.

TEN

Sell High, Sell Fast, Move On

This final chapter identifies common mistakes our clients find themselves making and summarises the solutions, bringing together the advice in the earlier chapters.

Top three vendor problems

- They need to sell quickly for maximum value.

- They don't know how/understand why/have time to make the house marketable.

- They don't want to spend any money to achieve a sale.

Seven mistakes vendors make in their thinking

- It's easy to sell a house.

- People will buy a house regardless of how it looks in photos and videos on the property portals.

- It's possible to achieve top money for a house without tidying up.

- Their house is worth more than it is.

- Because they love the quirky space, everyone else will.

- Dropping the price is the only way to get a buyer.

- A buyer will come along eventually.

Seven mistakes vendors make in their actions

- They don't target their ideal buyer.

- They don't prepare the house adequately ahead of marketing.

- They launch to the market with an overvaluation.

- They drop the guide price without considering alternatives.

- They don't look at their own home with a critical eye as a capital asset to be realised.

- They wait out the market, accepting political and economic uncertainty as a reason for their home not selling.

- They have an emotional attachment to their house and can't understand why viewers don't feel the same way about it as they do.

Why are these actions mistakes?

- Their buyer is likely to be a generation younger than they are or may be a young family moving up to an aspirational home. Their buyer is buying in a world which markets everything except houses (in the UK).

- Their buyer is looking at images of beautiful homes on other platforms – Instagram, Facebook, Houzz, Pinterest. The reality of looking at real homes on Rightmove is depressing.

- The housing market is difficult and estate agents are competing for business. Any agent who is prepared to value high and charge low fees is desperate, not giving good advice.

- Traditionally, the thing to do when a property didn't sell within the first few weeks, three months maximum, was to drop the price. In the UK, there wasn't much alternative. Many people still believe this to be the case and are simply unaware that presentation will often make more difference to attracting viewings, and therefore offers, than price. Spending money on a house when it's being sold is an investment. We have a lot of evidence and many case studies that show exactly how making this investment can pay off much more rapidly and effectively than dropping the price.

- People forget that not everyone can see past the clutter of twenty years' worth of family life and that their viewers often want the whole picture. They forget that their major investment is in their home but also that they have lived in it for many years. They often think their house is worth more and their expectations of realising too much capital are often unrealistic.

- The housing market is significantly affected by political and economic factors, but there are always people who need to sell and buy as their circumstances change. The best houses will continue to attract good offers even when the market is difficult.

- At the point of selling, a house must stop being tied to emotions. It's a capital asset creating the pathway to the next life stage.

Solutions to enable you to sell high, sell fast, move on

- Consider who you were when you bought the home you're now selling. Who do you expect your buyer to be?

- Engage your estate agent based on the good advice they give you, not on who's giving you the cheapest fees. An agent selling a home cheaply won't be able to invest the time with you to get the best sale.

- Enable the win-win-win situation for vendor, buyer and agent with a beautiful home for sale at a fair guide price.

- Prepare your house well ahead of your sale. Use our seven-step ADDRESS system to ensure you cover everything.

- Don't accept an estate agent's advice to drop the price on your home until you have investigated alternatives. Is it in fact the price that's the problem? Will changing the presentation make a bigger difference than dropping the price, and cost less?

- To what extent is the investment in home staging a risk? If you are stuck on the market then there will be a cost either in taking a price drop or in staging. A price drop always amounts to more than a sum of money spent on professional presentation. Compare prices of similar properties that have sold recently in your area. If your price is similar, this probably isn't the issue. The investment in professional home staging is less of a risk.

- Do you need to move now? If not, and you genuinely think that housing market uncertainty is your main problem, come off the market until you do need to move.

For more case studies, top tips and lots of advice, do visit our website www.lemonandlimeinteriors.co.uk. If we can give you advice or you would like a consultation with us, we would be delighted to hear from you. Good luck in selling your biggest capital asset for the best possible price!

Useful Resources

Books

Rae, C, Saunders Marsh, J, *Home Staging: The winning way to sell your house for more money* (Wiley, 2006)

Capelluto, A, *Home Staging for Dummies* (Wiley, 2008)

Capelluto, A, *The Power of Staging: a seller's guide to home staging* (International School Of Staging, 2016)

Websites

The Home Staging Association of UK and Ireland:

www.homestaging.org.uk

Some of the property portals and estate agents' sites host blogs on preparing your home for sale from time to time.

Check out:

www.rightmove.co.uk/advice

www.zoopla.co.uk/discover

www.fineandcountry.com/interior-design/staging-and
-styling

www.lemonandlimeinteriors.co.uk

The sister website of Lemon and Lime Interiors includes
blogs and tips about all aspects of home selling:

www.howtosellmyhouse.co.uk

Acknowledgements

I now understand why acknowledgement pages sometimes go on forever. I'll try to keep it short.

Firstly, huge thanks to Daniel Priestley and my group on the KPI course – James Church, Nick Ruston, Scott Burgess and Gary Ellerd-Elliot – for starting me off on my book-writing journey and keeping me going through the tough bits.

Thanks to Rob Watson, my amazing partner, for all the coffee, late nights and endless support. And to my team at Lemon and Lime, especially Kirsty Fisher, who picked up the workload when I retreated into my book-writing cave yet again.

To my readers, especially Jayne Dowle, without whom my sentences would have rambled on forever.

And to my publishing team, Lucy McCarraher and Roger Waltham, for all the advice and encouragement and for actually helping me get this done!

Thank you!

The Author

Elaine Penhaul is the founder of leading home staging company Lemon and Lime Interiors. She specialises in achieving great sales for her clients at the upper end of the property market. The properties Lemon and Lime stage for sale generally achieve their maximum values up to three times faster than comparable properties on the market. Elaine has been quoted in many publications, including *Estate Agent Today*, *The Times* and *Luxury Interiors Magazine*. She has developed a business course and accreditation programme for home stagers alongside the Home Staging Association of the UK and Ireland. She is passionate about helping other stagers understand that the business is not just about arranging cushions but about selling properties as effectively as possible.

Elaine grew up on the coast in Norfolk and currently lives in rural Derbyshire. She still misses the sea and plans to return to the coast eventually. She loves the outdoor life, red wine and chocolate. Her lifelong passion outside work is sailing everything from small dinghies to big yachts. She especially loves to sail with her partner, Rob, and her four grown-up children on holiday, preferably in the Ionian Islands of Greece.

Visit, message or call me for all the advice you need:

- ⊕ www.lemonandlimeinteriors.co.uk
- ⓕ @lemonandlimeinteriors
- ⓧ @LandLInteriors
- ⊙ lemonandlimeinteriors
- ⓟ Lemon and Lime
- ⓱ Lemon and Lime Interiors

Printed in Great Britain
by Amazon

57403372R00102